D0200919

19 2017

Praise for *Big Love*

"Has there ever been a more crucial time for *Big Love* to be released into our world? Scott Stabile is one of my favorite love artists and activists. His voice in this vital new book is fresh and relevant — his message urgent and universal. Scott is a force for love in a time when we are all desperate for healing. I look to Scott for wisdom and leadership, and he has delivered both with *Big Love*. This book opened my heart and mind, and I'm forever grateful."

— GLENNON DOYLE MELTON, author of
#1 *New York Times*–bestseller *Love Warrior*
and founder of *Momastery* and *Together Rising*

"Scott Stabile is a wonderful presence of love, advocacy, warmth, resilience, and grace in our world. I adore and admire everything he creates."

— ELIZABETH GILBERT, bestselling author of *Eat, Pray, Love*

"At the end of life, the core question we ask is, *Was I well loved and did I love well?* Scott Stabile doesn't wait to ask this fundamental question — love is already the center of his solar system. *Big Love* is an operating manual for living a heart-centered life in good times and bad. I've never read a more poignant and powerful ode to the power of love."

— CHIP CONLEY, bestselling author of
Peak and *Emotional Equations*

"*Big Love*, big heart, big opportunity to bring way more love into your life and consciousness with buoyancy, beauty, and boldness. Infinite love to Scott Stabile for bringing this everloving book into being."

— SARK, artist and coauthor of *Succulent Wild Love*

"*Big Love* is heartbreaking, hilarious, and entirely real. I saw parts of myself in every one of Scott's stories, and that is perhaps the greatest gift of this book — that he writes so openly about the struggles so many of us experience but hesitate to express, and he does so with incredible compassion, insight, and authenticity."

— MIKE ROBBINS, author of *Be Yourself, Everyone Else Is Already Taken*

"*Big Love* is one of those rare gems that spares us the pretension of light-and-fluffy love rhetoric and instead truly guides readers in how to love themselves and others without holding back. Thank you for this gift, Scott."

— CHRIS GROSSO, author of *Indie Spiritualist*, *Everything Mind*, and *Dead Set on Living*

"*Big Love* does something that many books strive for but fail to achieve. It cracks open the happy image of its author, Scott Stabile, and reveals the heartbreaking, life-altering realities that have shaped this man and what he teaches. Leading by example with this book, Scott shows what it means to live wide open and how vulnerability is true power."

— JACOB NORDBY, author of *Blessed Are the Weird: A Manifesto for Creatives*

BIG
LOVE

BIG LOVE

The Power of Living

——— *with* ———

a Wide-Open Heart

SCOTT STABILE

New World Library
Novato, California

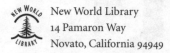 New World Library
14 Pamaron Way
Novato, California 94949

Text design by Tona Pearce Myers

Library of Congress Cataloging-in-Publication data is available.

First printing, September 2017
ISBN 978-1-60868-493-9
Ebook ISBN 978-1-60868-494-6
Printed in Canada on 100% postconsumer-waste recycled paper

 New World Library is proud to be a Gold Certified Environmentally Responsible Publisher. Publisher certification awarded by Green Press Initiative. www.greenpressinitiative.org

10   9   8   7   6   5   4   3   2   1

For my sisters,
Rose, Stacey, and Kim,
three loves of my life

● ● ●

CONTENTS

AUTHOR'S NOTE

On a scale from 1 to 10 — with 1 being an empty void and 10 being an elephant — my memory rests somewhere between a 6 and a 7. And it's trending downward. Luckily, the stories I've chosen to convey here are nestled closer to the elephant zone, a good thing when you're writing a book of personal essays built on memories. I've done my best to retell everything as accurately as possible and have made note if a piece of any story remains blurry. Though I have not conveyed conversations verbatim, I've locked onto their essence and, in some cases, a lot of the actual words spoken. Also, I've changed a bunch of names — of people and locations — but only to keep anonymity intact and not because I don't remember the real ones.

INTRODUCTION

About fifteen years ago a good friend asked me, "What do you want to do with your life?" Doesn't that question drive you nuts? That was hardly the first time I'd been asked it, and I'd never had a suitable answer that felt connected to some clear destiny or deep longing. Yes, there was a time in middle school when I desperately wanted to be a professional tennis player, even though I wasn't especially good at the sport. The longing was there, though; I played and fantasized about tennis constantly and saw myself battling Boris Becker on the grasses of Wimbledon. My passion for tennis faded through high school, since I preferred to imagine myself onstage with Bono, belting out "Desire." As a generally directionless adult, I'd always envied my professional friends who had known since childhood exactly how they wanted to spend their time as grown-ups. I never had a clue.

"Really, what do you want to do with your life?" my friend pressed, when I still hadn't answered him.

I'd like to never have to answer this question again, that's what, I thought.

I bypassed the impulse to say *travel the world* and *just be happy*, trusting I could summon a little more depth in my answer. "I want to spread as much love as possible," I responded. Cue the rainbows and unicorns! Can I get a puppy over here?

I'm not sure my answer was deep, but it was the truth.

"Okay," my friend replied, "how do you want to do that?" Pain in the ass, that friend.

"I have no idea," I said. That was the truth, too. I didn't know exactly what the role of love-spreader entailed, but it felt like a life goal to which I could commit myself, one that came with an important benefit our world desperately needed — love, love, and more love. More than anything, I believed in love, and in the power of love to create important, positive change. I still believe that, as much as ever.

Seriously, what's not to love about love?

Love makes the most difference in every area that matters. It always has, and it always will.

We can all be love-spreaders, by the way, if we choose to be. You don't even need to quit your day job. Every time we act with kindness or acceptance, we spread love. Every time we choose compassion over condemnation, we spread love. Every time we find the courage to forgive, we spread love. Life presents us with daily opportunities to share a little, or a whole lotta love. Every single time we do, an angel sprouts new wings and cries silver tears of joy. Okay, that angel thing doesn't really happen, but we do absolutely serve ourselves and our world through love.

Isn't that reason enough to love more? I think so.

It was with fame rather than love in mind that I launched my Facebook author page in 2012. I wanted to promote both a kids' movie and a young adult paranormal romance I'd written. As it turned out, the crowds didn't flock to either. After some feeble attempts at self-promotion, along with the realization that marketing myself made me anxious / want to vomit, I changed the direction of the page. The question, *What do you want to do with your life?* became, *What do you want to do with this page?* I came up with the same answer: spread some love.

I decided to make my page a home of positivity, a Polly-anna's paradise. I began posting about the subjects that mattered most to me, such as kindness, compassion, forgiveness, authenticity and, of course, love. I happy-memed the hell out of that page, and people started to notice. The page took off — hundreds and then thousands began showing up — and I was deliriously excited to have found another outlet for my love-spreading desires. My ego, incidentally, felt equally excited to be getting *likes* all the time.

Being in the heart-and-soul meme business can get tricky, however. How many different ways could one communicate the meaning of life — or *a* meaning of life — in a sentence or two? There weren't enough creative fonts and nature backgrounds on the planet to make everything I wrote compelling. Or unique. I knew that. We self-help, spirituality, personal-development types are all saying the same things, more or less: kindness matters, compassion is king (or queen), love wins, just be yourself. These are good things to say, I think. Important reminders. But are they enough?

I thought so, until a woman commented beneath one of my standard *life is so beautiful and we're all blessed to be here* posts: "Not everybody is as happy and positive as you are all the time, Scott. Some of us are really struggling." That comment hurt — not just because I considered myself a particularly moody person who struggled plenty, but also because my happy words had provoked her to feel worse instead of better, "less than" instead of equal. That sucked. Of course, based on what I'd been posting on my page, she had no reason to see me as anything but a smiling *Pollymanna*. Why would she see us as the same?

So I started to share myself. For real.

I wrote about growing up with a brother addicted to heroin and grieving my parents, who were murdered when I was fourteen. I posted about the shame I carried for years over being gay, and my struggle to be authentic in a world that wants us to be anything but. I wrote about my fears and insecurities, my sadness and rage, and the ways in which I was working through the darker parts of my life in order to create more space for the light. Don't panic; my page didn't suddenly turn all gloom and doom. There was still a lot of *love rocks* and *gratitude is the fastest path to happiness* going on. I just let myself be more honest, and more vulnerable. The community that gathered around the page responded in kind, and suddenly many of us felt a lot less alone — in our idiosyncrasies and in our pain. Some version of *I feel better knowing I'm not the only one* became one of the most common comments I'd see. Honesty and vulnerability are nothing but love in action, after all.

Shortly after I began writing this book, I stood in front of the mirror and asked myself, "What do you want *Big Love* to do?" An important question, the answers to which I have no control over. A man can hope, though, so…

I'd like this book to remind you that you are not alone, not by a long shot. We are all imperfect; we all have busy, fearful minds; and we all struggle. Every single one of us, every single day. I'd like the book to emphasize that you are as worthy of love as anyone who has ever lived, and that nothing you do could ever make you any less worthy. Or *more* worthy, for that matter. I'd like it to encourage you to take responsibility for every aspect of your life, knowing that by empowering yourself this way, you set yourself up for deeper peace and greater joy. I'd like it to open you up to perspectives you may not have considered, or reinforce ones you may have forgotten, all of which will lead to a more open and honest relationship with yourself and others. Most important, I'd like this book to inspire you to consider love as the guiding force in your life, regardless of circumstance. Nothing stands to transform us, our relationships, and our world, more than a commitment to live our lives from love. The bigger the better.

Oh, and I hope you laugh more than a little, and I'd like the book to sell at least a million copies.

That's what *I'd* like. What about you? What brings you to *Big Love*?

Perhaps you've picked it up because you're a fan of my Facebook page and want to see if I can actually communicate in more than memes. Or perhaps you love the cover and, like me, sometimes choose books and wine bottles solely because of their pretty labels. It works for me at least 25 percent of the time! Maybe you're just a fan of love, and the bigger the better, so *Big Love* makes for an obvious choice. Or you thought this book was about that HBO polygamist series with the same name and you still haven't figured out it's not. (Sorry about that.) Maybe, like so many of us, you're having a hard time making sense of our unpredictable reality, and you're searching for words, ideas, and people with whom you can connect and from whom you might learn a thing or three. I am, too. Always. We all want to feel a bit more hopeful, and a lot less alone.

Whatever your reason, I'm happy you're here. Grateful, too. Thank you, thank you, thank you. I forded a river of insecurities and fears to write this book (paging Mr. Drama), and it's an honor to share it with you. A dream come true, really. That said, just to manage your expectations, I'm absolutely certain the answers to all life's challenges are not contained within the pages of this book. I'm also somewhat certain that some answers to some of life's challenges (some of the time) are contained here — at least answers that have helped me find more peace, joy, and meaning. Answers that often begin and end with love. Since we're all so similar — once you dig beneath the surface to our human insecurities, fears, and joys — I'm confident some of these answers, as well as many of the questions I pose, will resonate with you in some way. We don't have to live each other's stories to understand each other's lives. If the lovely people in my social media community have taught me anything, it's that we're pretty much all the same, and we each have so much to learn from one another.

We all want to give and receive love.

We all want to be seen.

I see you, by the way, and you're positively radiant.

In each chapter of this book, I share a personal experience that pulled me from my center — that shook me up — and the ways in which I brought myself back to peace, and to love. Some of the experiences are tragic, like my parents' murder in 1985, and my brother's heroin overdose nine years later. In those chapters you won't likely be snickering at my clever delivery (assuming you've snickered at all so far). Making my way back to center has entailed integrating those realities into my life rather than finding any real closure with them. Does anyone honestly find closure with grief?

Most of the stories, however, reflect on everyday challenges we can all relate to, like the weight of shame, the search for happiness, the struggle to be authentic, and the awkwardness of sperm donation. (Well, maybe you can't relate to that one.) I look at situations that provoked my mind to do its crazy dance, which just happens to be my mind's favorite way to boogie. Throughout these chapters, I focus on the many mandates of love, such as kindness, compassion, acceptance, and forgiveness. I consider what happens when we choose love over fear, the heart over the ego. (Spoiler alert: really good stuff.) I don't shy away from the times I've acted like a total asshole, either. In fact, they make perfect examples of how much harder life is when we operate outside the energy of love. (Spoiler alert #2: way harder.)

Though I knew I wanted the book's title to be *Big Love* — because I love those two words together *and* because that's my most common sign-off to my Facebook community — I wasn't sure it captured the content well enough. Then I considered all the different examples I share in these pages, all the ways in which I've struggled to be compassionate or forgiving or gracious or kind. The instances of overwhelming envy or self-righteousness, the moments of embarrassing failure and shame. In each instance, it was love that carried me back to my center. Love encouraged me to show up for my life authentically. Love challenged me to move forward, despite my fears. Every single time, love walked me home.

The one thing I know for sure:

Love makes life better. Love heals.

Okay, that's two things, but you get the picture.

Choose love for a week, and see if your life doesn't feel different. That's homework, by the way, so get to it. Every time you're inclined to act from anger or blame or self-righteousness or condemnation, stop yourself, take a good, long breath, and invite love into the moment. Just to see what happens. I'm betting on something great. Even miraculous.

This feels like a good time to get to the actual book. (Unless you're here for the HBO series and still haven't figured out you're in the wrong place. Or are you?)

Before we dive in, I want to give a shout-out to my Facebook community. I wish I could blast trumpets for them. I have no doubt that this book exists, in great part, because of the love and support they've shown me the past few years — and because there are a lot of them, which made me that much more appealing to my publisher. They've kept me inspired to show up, to keep writing, and to share my truth.

They've helped me through some dark moments and have reminded me — when I really needed the reminder — that I am not alone, and that I am loved. They've encouraged me to keep moving forward and to create a life that more closely reflects my dreams. (It's happening!) I'm so very grateful for their belief in me.

To you reading this right now, whoever and wherever you are, I hope you never doubt that you are beautiful, resilient, and so very worthy of love, just as you are. Thank you for going on this journey with me. May we get lost in hope, inspiration, clarity, connection, fun and, of course, BIG LOVE.

DIG

I was fourteen when my parents were shot and killed in their Detroit fruit market. Mary's Market. That's what the sign said when they bought the store many years before, so they stuck with the name. All their customers called my mom Mary, even though her name was Camille. She never corrected them. My dad, James, was Jimmy to all. Jimmy and Camille Stabile. Fifty-eight and fifty-six years old. Married for thirty-seven years. Parents to seven children. Murdered on a Monday morning in September.

I had spent that weekend at my sister Rose's house. We had just finished breakfast when my brother Jimmy called to tell her that a neighbor had spotted our parents' empty navy-blue Camaro parked outside their market. The market's doors were still closed and locked, hours after they should have been opened. Nobody inside was answering the phone.

I saw my sister's panic and felt my own. My parents' store was in a rough neighborhood of Detroit, too familiar with violent crime, and nothing about this situation seemed right.

Where are you? I thought. *Just answer the phone and tell us you're okay*. I feared the worst but chose to stay hopeful until we knew what had happened. It's difficult enough to accept a loved one's death when it's certain, impossible to do so when there's any doubt. Without confirmation, my parents stayed alive in my mind. Barely.

Rose and I hurried to her brown Chevy Chevette and headed to her husband, Joe's, restaurant — the Ham Palace — where he and my sister Kim worked. We would gather there while Jimmy drove to my parents' store to find out what was going on. I don't recall what Rose and I talked about, if anything, during the ride. All I remember is the "Love Theme from St. Elmo's Fire" playing on the radio. Other songs must have played during the twenty-five minutes it took for us to get to the Ham Palace, but I recall only that saxophone-soaked instrumental. It was the soundtrack to those final, hopeful thoughts of a future life with my parents and will forever be the song I associate with losing them.

My brother-in-law closed the restaurant early, and he, Rose, Kim, and I, along with Lori, a family friend who worked there, waited for news about my parents. My mind raced between hope and fear, between possibility and dread, between a simple misunderstanding and a life-changing nightmare. I had just stepped out of the bathroom when my brother Jimmy arrived. I stopped at the bathroom door and watched, from across the restaurant, as he spoke words I couldn't hear to my sisters. Then came their screams. Those I heard clearly. Rose and Kim collapsed into each other's arms and wailed. And hope vanished.

I slipped back into the dark bathroom, crouched in the corner beside the urinal, and sobbed to the sound of my sisters' screams. To this day, I have still never felt as alone as I did that day in the bathroom. I wanted my sisters to hold me, too. I wanted to insert myself into their grip, but I couldn't make myself go out there. I couldn't walk into that reality, and so I stayed, on the piss-stained floor, alone. Lost. Shocked and shaking. I heard Rose ask, "Where's Scott?" just before Lori walked in, knelt down beside me, and wrapped me in her arms. She held me as if I were her son, and she cried along with me.

The police would report that my parents had arrived at the market to find two men inside — their friend and employee, T, who had been stabbed, as well as the man who stabbed him. My father called 911 to get help for T, and when the operator asked my dad if he knew who did it, he replied something to the effect of, "No, but there's a man here who might." My parents were shot soon after the 911 call. The homicide inspector would say that the man who stabbed, and ultimately killed, T did so in a "fit of anger" over a money dispute and that he killed my parents because they could identify him. Their killer was a regular customer at the store.

A police cruiser arrived at the market within minutes of my dad's 911 call, but the officers left because the doors were locked and they believed the store to be empty. Three hours would pass before neighbors called the police again, because the store still hadn't opened. You can waste a life wondering what might have happened had those first officers gone inside and called an ambulance. Or you can convince yourself that your parents would have died anyway, even if help had arrived, that their injuries were too extreme. One thing you cannot do is erase the image of them bloodied and dead on the floor of their fruit market, the market where you had spent many summer and weekend days working alongside them.

● ● ●

I had no idea how to process my parents' deaths, let alone the way they died. How does a fourteen-year-old wrap his mind around such violence, and such loss? How does anyone? After a foggy couple of months punctuated by seesawing shock and devastation, I locked their deaths — and their lives — away, deep within me, out of reach of my day-to-day existence.

I moved in with Rose (who was thirty at the time) and Joe and their son, my nephew Joey. I went from my ethnically diverse westside suburb to her strictly white and Christian eastside neighborhood. I started a new high school, immersed myself in schoolwork, and acted like everything was just fine. Like I didn't miss my old home and school desperately. Like I was adjusting well to my new reality. Like I wasn't an orphan whose mom and dad had been murdered just months before. I smiled a lot, made a bunch of new friends, and mastered the art of shifting any discussion about parents to some other topic.

"What does your dad do for work?" a classmate would ask.

"Wait, have you heard the new Tears for Fears song?" I would respond. And just like that, we'd be talking about music.

Like a pro chess player, always several moves ahead, I

manipulated most conversations away from family well before they even landed on the subject. This vigilance taxed me,
but I refused to let my new classmates know about my parents.
I wanted to appear normal at all costs, and ninth-grade orphans weren't the norm in suburban Detroit.

I kept myself busy throughout high school — as the
class president, as the student council vice president, as the
school board liaison, as a yearbook editor, as a tennis player,
as a swimmer, as a clerk at the local sporting goods store, as
a receptionist at an area tennis club, as a popular and smart
kid with more than enough school, work, and social distractions to ensure as little parental contemplation as possible. I
thought about my parents every day, of course, but I didn't
allow myself to dwell on their absence. I didn't allow myself
to *feel* them. And I definitely didn't talk about them. My siblings, like me, never talked about my parents, either, which
only made it easier to keep Mom and Dad locked away.

After high school, I leapt into life as a college kid at the
University of Michigan. I made lots of new friends, partied a
bunch, joined a fraternity, partied even more, worked several
jobs, skipped the classes that bored me, excelled in the ones
that enthralled me, transitioned from a Republican to a leftist
revolutionary, quit the fraternity, tried most drugs for the first
time, had a good amount of sex, and generally loved my four
years in Ann Arbor.

Through it all, I continued to hide the fact that I was an
orphan as much as I could. I eventually told my close friends,
of course, but kept it quiet with everyone else. I felt ashamed
to have lost my parents the way I did. Like I was deeply flawed,

even cursed, because of their murder. Besides, college-aged orphans may have been slightly more common, but the murderous backstory overwhelmed people. And their shocked *oh my Gods* and sad *I'm so sorrys* overwhelmed *me*. Even more than feeling like a freak, I didn't want to be pitied by my peers, and it's impossible not to feel pity for someone whose parents were shot to death. So I continued to act like everything was okay. And, for the most part, it was.

About once a year throughout high school and college, triggered by an unexpected conversation or too many drinks or the sheer inability to suppress the grief anymore, I'd sob myself raw for hours and hours and then get back to being fine.

This was how I coped. How I survived. I disconnected from the reality of my parents' death. I buried the pain. The truth is, I didn't consciously do anything. It's as though the pain buried itself to protect me, to keep me from burying myself beneath it.

But the pain didn't really go away. It stayed hidden but present, like a parasite. Not enough to take me down but enough to weaken me. It entered my body in the form of a regular cough and a nervous stomach. It entered my relationships as controlled distance and an unwillingness to commit too seriously to anyone. It entered my sleep as nightmares, endless scenarios of violence and death. Because I wouldn't allow for its release, the emotional pain created outlets of its own, however it could.

Still, into my twenties, I acted like I had dealt with my parents' death and moved on. What else was there to do? I was so good at avoiding my grief, I had convinced myself it no longer existed. I wasn't pretending I was okay; in my mind, I was healed. I didn't attribute my nervous stomach or my fear of intimacy to losing my parents. I shook off any suggestion of abandonment issues, even after ending yet another relationship too suddenly and without good reason. Aside from the constant nightmares, in which my parents or I were being chased and murdered, I didn't believe their death was affecting my life much at all.

I was wrong.

In my early twenties and living in San Francisco, I had one of my yearly cries. Except it lasted for days. I locked myself in my bedroom and unraveled. All the pain I'd been hiding revealed itself. Rage and devastation and hopelessness swallowed me. I couldn't stop thinking about my parents, grasping for any memories that my grief hadn't vanquished. Mom, in her purple terry-cloth jumpsuit and oversize glasses, stirring her pasta sauce, a lit cigarette dangling from her lips. Dad stretched out on the family room sofa, eating popcorn from his favorite aluminum bowl, watching *Star Trek*. The two weeks every summer we spent at the log cabin in northern Michigan. Hours upon hours of pinochle and poker games.

Along with the memories, I focused on their murders, as though I had been there. I heard the gunshots and my mother's screams. I saw my parents drop to the floor, as blood pooled around their bodies. I pictured their killer standing over them, his gun still cocked, ready to take another shot just to be sure. These images played like loops in my mind — the screams, the bodies, the blood, their killer — and I couldn't make them stop. I wondered about their last breaths. *Could they see each other at the end? What were their final words to each other? Did Mom think of me at all?*

Then came my anger, an impossible rage, and it didn't target just God, though it hit God hard. It went after my parents, too. Why did my dad have to buy that fucked-up market in that fucked-up neighborhood? How could he ever have allowed my mom to work there? And why didn't she say no? The week they got killed was to be my mom's last week at the store. For months I'd been begging her to quit, and she had finally relented. Four more days, and she would have been free. Just ninety-six more hours. Then my anger moved on from my parents and went after me. Why hadn't I begged her harder? Why hadn't *I* made her quit months before? I could have saved her life.

Still locked in my room in San Francisco, I kept mourning. I hated my parents, then loved them, then missed them, then blamed them. More than anything, I just wanted them back. I wanted more time with them. No longer in denial, I had finally woken up — to a nightmare. I couldn't see a future beyond the pain. I didn't consider suicide, yet I couldn't find the point in living with so much anger and sadness. I had no idea how to move forward.

My sobs continued. I started to worry I was losing my mind, that something had cracked inside me and that I wouldn't be able to stop crying. I've never felt closer to a complete mental breakdown. In a panic, or perhaps a moment of clarity, I pulled out the Yellow Pages to find a psychologist. I closed my eyes and pointed blindly at a name, then called the number. She saw me two days later. Once a week for six weeks we talked, mostly about my parents — something I hadn't done in the nine years since they'd been dead. I shared and cried and raged and cried some more. Those six sessions were all I could afford at the time, but they grounded me again. They marked a beginning. They opened me up to the possibility of talking about my parents without going crazy, something I think I subconsciously feared during all those years in denial.

It took breaking down to open up. Reaching out to go within. Losing my resistance to find my strength. I had finally started digging up the pain I'd buried so deeply, for so long. In fits and spurts, at times casually, at times relentlessly, I've been digging ever since.

● ● ●

Not long after I stopped seeing the therapist, I started a job at New Moon, an unapologetically New Age gift shop in the Upper Haight district of San Francisco. New Moon looked like a hippie art show, smelled like Indian incense, sounded like African drums, tasted like free-trade chocolate, and felt like home.

Conversations that reached well below the surface weren't just welcomed at New Moon, they were expected. I quickly befriended my coworkers, many of whom viewed their spiritual path — especially the pursuit of enlightenment — as the most important part of their lives. I had never even heard of enlightenment or considered my spiritual path at that point, at least not consciously. That changed fast. I adored these new friends, and I couldn't get enough of their peace-and-love vibe, so I asked them lots of questions about consciousness and enlightenment and what it took to grow spiritually. Among the many responses, one idea stood out consistently: along with a committed focus on love, a necessary component of spiritual growth was a direct and honest confrontation with your pain. You can't live in denial and expect to grow. Smiling through life only gets you so far.

Between these new, deep friendships and my instant obsession with the self-help and spirituality book sections of the store, I opened, for the first time, to working on my healing in an active way. Which basically meant just being honest about my pain and not too afraid to face it some of the time. I welcomed the long-overdue reflection on my parents' death and how it had impacted my life. I invited a good cry much more often than once a year. I read about self-love and loss, acceptance and surrender, forgiveness and personal responsibility. I talked openly with my closest work friends about my life, my parents, my fears, and my insecurities. We shared everything with each other. I learned how important it is to share your story with those you can trust to listen without judgment, and to listen to the stories of others with compassion and understanding. This open dialogue reminded me that we all have lives marked by struggle, and it helped me to keep digging into my own pockets of pain. My friends supported me as I faced my past and helped me to feel I wasn't facing it alone.

My experience at New Moon, along with the connection I developed with a local spiritual teacher, opened me up to living my life differently, with compassion and love as primary goals, with spiritual growth as my purpose. I began to long for enlightenment, and enlightenment, as I came to understand it, didn't happen without diving into your pain. Not keeping it buried, not skirting around it, not denying it's there, but heading directly into and through it, as courageously as possible. We can't honestly address what we're not willing to honestly face. It's common sense, really. And a hard truth, for sure.

● ● ●

I was interviewed for the *Home* podcast recently, and one of the hosts asked me if it was still difficult to talk about what happened to my parents, all these years later. I told her, "Usually no, but sometimes, yes." It depends on the context of the conversation and how I'm feeling right then. Even today, at times, more than thirty years later, I'm heavy with grief over the fact that they're gone and the way they died. I mourn for the brutality of their deaths and the fear they must have felt in those final moments. I mourn for the relationship I never got to have with them as a teenager and adult, and for everything they never got to experience with me. I mourn being an orphan. I mourn the unfairness of it all.

What's so much different now that I'm older is that I allow the grief to enter, and stay as long as it needs, even when it's darkening my mind and ripping at my heart. Even when the pain of it scares me. I don't pretend I'm not feeling it, and usually (but not always) don't distract myself to keep from taking in its fullness. Eventually, it moves through me. That's how emotions are designed. They let go of us when we stop hold-ing on to them. And I don't live my life anymore as though I'm keeping a big secret or running from a deeper truth. I'm no longer ashamed of my past. That freedom alone makes feeling the pain worth it.

We're all living with emotional pain — often deep pain — and whether or not we do it consciously, many of us bury much of it inside. Where it feeds freely on our potential for happiness. Where it keeps us from opening up to the breadth of our truth. Where it prevents us from living within the beauty of our freedom. Buried but present. Always present.

Maybe it's time to dig some of it up?

We all have our reasons for burying our pain, but at the core it comes down to fear. Fear of facing the truth of what we've done or endured, the truth of just how dark our dark-ness is, and the fear that we can't survive it. That it will destroy us. But it won't. Whatever it is, we can survive it; we've *already* survived it.

But what if now is the time to do more than simply sur-vive? What if now is the time to live in a more conscious, de-liberate way? What if now is the time to let the healing begin, for real?

Healing isn't possible within denial and fear. It's only pos-sible within openness and honesty, within our willingness to look at the truth of our reality, past and present, and to accept it for what it is without letting it define who we are right now. We are not our struggles, or our heartbreak. We are not the actions we've taken, or the assaults we've endured. Yes, our experiences influence how we grow and who we grow into.

But ultimately, who we are is who we decide to be, because of and despite everything we've been through. Our power lives in choice. We *can* choose to face our pain without judgment, without letting it shut us down to our growth. If we decide to. And we can commit to loving ourselves through it all. As much as possible, no matter what. Love — self-love — transforms. This is how we create a safe place inside ourselves, to heal.

When I started to allow for the pain of losing my parents, I didn't just awaken to profound levels of grief that needed to be felt so that it could be released. I was also able to see how their death — by far the most tragic and transformative event in my life — has helped me grow into a more independent, compassionate, and loving man than I might have been otherwise. I'm not at all thankful they died, and I could never view their murders as a blessing, but I am grateful to have grown stronger because of their death. And I hope that my resilience helps others to see that growth and healing are possible, regardless of circumstance. There are gifts in even our greatest sorrows, if we're willing to acknowledge them. If we're willing to work at seeing them.

As a guy who posts lots of pretty pictures with quotes about being yourself and seeking happiness and love, love, love, I need to be clear about something: it's easy to say *just be* or *just love*, and my experience with those realities — though still more limited than I would like — is powerful beyond measure, but getting there is difficult. One of the hardest things we're likely to attempt in our lifetime. Staying there is even harder. It takes more than just wanting to be blissed out on peace and love, or we'd all be gurus. It takes work. Hard, important, necessary work.

Much of that work begins and ends with our pain. It begins and ends in those painful truths we try to ignore, the ones so many of us have masterfully buried. The sooner we take out our shovels and start to dig, the sooner we invite into our lives a new kind of hope, a new taste of freedom. It's not easy. It hurts, but it's worth it. It's so worth it.

What does that work look like? It looks like whatever it takes to get us to feel, reflect on, and accept whatever we've seen, done, or experienced, as well as the reality of our lives in the present. For some, meditation works, or therapy, or yoga, or self-help books, or art. For others, it's support groups, or ayahuasca journeys, or music, or a combination of several or all these things, and so much more. It comes down to figuring out what works for us and giving our intention and energy to it.

I use writing as a tool to process my pain. The act of spilling my thoughts and feelings onto a page, whether or not that page is to be seen by others, offers me a powerful and important outlet for my darkness. I read books, listen to podcasts, and watch talks that inspire me to open up a little more, to dig a little deeper. I dance my ass off all the time in my apartment to release energy. I engage in difficult conversations with my partner and family and friends to work through issues and to grow both personally and interpersonally. I connect with my social media communities, especially on Facebook, to share my experiences in an honest way with others who want to share their stories and work at creating the possibility of healing themselves. Others who want to dig rather than keep things buried.

I don't do all these things all the time. Who wants to have difficult conversations every day? Not me. Sometimes I just melt into the sofa, lose myself in TV, and shovel chips and ice cream into my mouth. Sometimes I hide, or escape, or numb myself for a bit. But I always resurface and get back to work, because I'm dedicated to my spiritual growth, and to my happiness. I'm dedicated to myself.

Beyond everything else, growth requires dedication. Healing demands commitment. No number of books or podcasts or workshops will make a difference if we're not committed to healing ourselves. And when we open ourselves to look at our pain for real, our pain will present itself. For real. It's usually not a very pretty picture. I continue to learn things about myself that I wish weren't true. I see new depths to my anger, and envy, and sadness. New proof all the time that I can be much less kind and generous than I desire and a much bigger asshole than I'd ever want to be. The work of awareness and consciousness is a process, and it's endless.

I'm certain I still haven't unburied all the pain around my parents' death, or the pain I carry regarding my relationship with them while they were alive. I never liked my dad, and though I loved my mom, I resented both my parents for their lack of interest in my life. I wanted them to care more about me. I wanted them to see me. I may never expose all the wounds I've got around them, and that's okay. I'm making progress. I'm opening. I'm growing. This book is another exercise in digging, in sharing my story so that it might support deeper healing for myself, and maybe, if I'm lucky, inspire it in others. That's one of the many beautiful benefits of facing your pain: whether or not you intend to, you're likely to inspire others to look at their own pain more openly and courageously. Along with digging yourself into a more fully realized life, you end up passing out shovels to others, too.

I've been digging for a while now, and I'll continue to dig, because I want to invite any opportunity for deeper healing. I want to face the full expression of myself, past to present, with acceptance and love. Always more love. I need only to look at how far I've come to know it's possible. I need only to consider my life right now to understand the transformational power of this kind of work. I will continue to explore all the possibilities of my growth, and to live as truthfully as possible. Because I want, more than anything, to be free.

THE COUGHER

I had an unusually inspiring experience at the San Francisco airport. I was relaxing in one of the airline clubs, because I'm fancy like that, eating pasty oatmeal topped with stale granola out of a cardboard bowl (see, fancy). I was doing my best to drown out the CNN election coverage, when a room-shaking yet succinct cough exploded from somewhere near the self-service espresso counter. The sound was extraordinary, like something you'd expect to come out of a bear or an elephant or even Godzilla, but definitely not a human. A thunderous boom, it made me jump a little in my seat.

I studied my fellow club denizens but couldn't figure out who was behind the cough. Surely not the tanned, elderly woman dripping in diamonds and sipping her morning Chardonnay. She couldn't have produced such a sound. It wasn't the petite businesswoman, either, in a chocolate-brown pantsuit, typing away on her laptop in between bites of biscotti. All children were definitely out; this noise came from someone full-grown. But no one looked embarrassed or guilty or like a radioactive monster on layover from Tokyo. It was as though it hadn't happened at all, like I had imagined the sound. Until it happened again, the same exact expulsion, every bit as enormous as the first one. This time, however, I was looking right at the culprit when he let loose — an older man, probably in his early seventies, casually dressed, reading *USA Today*, completely unfazed by the blare that had just exploded from his body. So unfazed was he that he didn't even bother to cover his mouth. He let go right into the sports section.

For the next half hour, as I finished my oatmeal, downed two mini-muffins, and started on a bagel (because, free food), the man let out his monstrous cough about every minute. Like clockwork. If it was possible to hide his cough, or at least downsize it to a lower level on the Richter scale, he showed no interest in doing so. I had no idea what he was thinking, of course, but he didn't appear bothered by the cough at all, or even, more incredibly, the least bit self-conscious about it. I wasn't the only one alarmed by his sonic boom, either. More than a few people cleared the area after a couple of rounds. The tanned, elderly woman practically sprinted out of there, wine in hand. The cougher, however, just sipped his coffee and read his paper as he violently hacked his way through the morning. This was clearly his norm.

When the man got up to leave, he walked right by me and smiled a kind, sincere smile. I nodded and smiled back. Little did he know, in the short time I had listened to and watched him cough, he'd inspired me in a profound way. He became my airport club hero that morning. I still think about him and his cough regularly. Which sounds strange, of course, if you don't know the reason why.

Hello. My name is Scott, and I'm a cougher. I cough all the time. Not just cough, either. I sniffle, clear my throat, swallow hard, and blow air out of my nose while making a *chee* sort of sound. I hem and ahem and snort and hack. In short, I make a whole lot of irritating noise with my nose, throat, and mouth, a symphony of gurgles and air and phlegm. Every day, throughout the day.

My *coughsnifflechee* is one of the things I'm most self-conscious about (nestled somewhere among my crooked teeth and back hair). Nobody likes to cough constantly, just as nobody likes a constant cougher. It's distracting, annoying, even fear inducing in closed spaces. In movie theaters, I cough. On airplanes, I clear my throat. In restaurants, I *ahem*. In yoga class, I sniffle. No matter where I am, I'm making unnecessary noise, and unlike my hero in the airport lounge, I'm always aware of my *coughsnifflechee* and the probability that others are, too.

I've coughed for most of my life. Though I can't pinpoint exactly when it started, my first memory of coughing with any sort of regularity was in high school, not long after my parents died. I don't think that's a coincidence. As far as I know, and I've seen doctors about it in the past, my cough isn't reflective of any physical ailment. That suggests it's emotional, or psychological, and I believe it is. When I get nervous, my *coughsnifflechee* goes haywire — before business dealings and unfamiliar social gatherings and important relationship conversations. Any time I'm the least bit insecure or uncertain of an outcome, I devolve into a hacking mess. Usually, and luckily, the extreme of this happens when I'm alone, before engaging in whatever it is that's induced my fit. Conversely, when I'm on vacation, completely relaxed, and especially when I'm immersed in nature of any kind, my cough relaxes. I can go days without coughing. Okay, not really. But a few hours, for sure.

About ten years ago, I stopped coughing, cold turkey. I pulled up to my favorite LA tennis court, about to go play a match, and told myself, "Enough with this cough. You're done. Now." And I was. I made it six months with no coughing. But I had to concentrate on not coughing *all the time*. Fighting back the coughs with my mind, swallowing them down instead of releasing them. It never became natural. It never felt good. All that effort proved more irritating than the cough, so I surrendered to my *coughsnifflechee*, and it's been with me ever since.

There are many *spiritual* explanations for coughing. One website I stumbled on states that *chronic coughing or gagging is the result of divine punishment coupled with a satanic attack*. Now, that's disheartening but might explain some of my recent nightmares if true. In the world of metaphysics, a cough suggests an imbalance in the throat chakra, the chakra associated with self-expression and communication. These imbalances are likely to occur when you're unable to say what you need to say, when you're having trouble expressing yourself. Since I often have trouble saying exactly what I want or need to say, especially when it's vulnerable, provocative, or potentially hurtful to do so, that rings truer than a satanic attack. Thank goodness. The cough, however, has never completely disappeared, even after I've mustered up the courage to speak some hard truths. In traditional Chinese medicine, every organ is associated with an emotion, and the lungs are the organ of sadness or grief. A persistent cough could represent grief that is suppressed or unexpressed. *Hmmm*. The cough began after my parents were killed. And I'm certain, even with all the grieving I've done over the years, there are suppressed pockets, possibly abysses, of grief still within me. I'm giving it to traditional Chinese medicine for the win.

I may not know exactly why I cough the way I do, but I do know how it's made me feel over the years: frustrated, scared, embarrassed, and ashamed. Frustrated because it's tiring and annoying to be coughing and clearing my throat all the time. Scared when my hypochondriac mind tells me I'm giving myself throat cancer or that my coughing will eventually swell up my throat until I can't breathe (clearly, my hypochondriac mind has never been to med school). Embarrassed because I know some people are thinking, "Geez, that guy makes a lot of noise. I hope he's not contagious." I'd be thinking the same. The shame, however, has been the hardest. Isn't it always?

My shame insists that my cough reflects some major character flaw, a weakness within me, something to be hidden at all costs. Especially because my cough appears to be solely emotional, which suggests I'm not nearly as emotionally sound as I, and the many thousands in my social media community, suspect me to be. What kind of personal growth teacher–type person can't even get himself together enough to stop coughing? What kind of healer can't heal himself? Shame uses my cough to convince me I'm a fraud. When I let it.

Like any senseless bully, my shame only grows stronger in my silence. It feeds on secrecy, on my unwillingness to acknowledge those things about which I feel guilty or regretful or humiliated. Shame tells me I'm unlovable — a flawed, vile monster — and that the world is unsafe, overflowing with people who want nothing more than to judge and condemn me for my appearance, and ideas, and choices. My shame tells me to hide.

I spent nearly every moment of my time in college underneath a baseball cap, to keep my fellow students — even my closest friends — from discovering that I was losing my hair. My shame told me my balding head wasn't just unusual at that age but also ugly and something to make fun of. I wasted so much emotional energy on my hair loss, and on keeping it hidden. I sat at the back of the computer center, facing the entrance, so that no one could walk up behind me and snatch off my cap, because, as we all know, college computer centers are hotbeds of cap-snatching. When I went to bed with a woman, I waited until we turned off the lights to take off my hat, and I kept her hands off my head at all times, lest she discover the secret of my baldness and run screaming from the bed. Even around my family, who had all watched my three older brothers go bald in their twenties, I kept my hat on. As though it were glued to my head. And during my waking hours, it was. Once I finally got over the shame of losing my hair — aided more by my move to San Francisco and the sudden popularity of shaved heads than by my enlightened realization that we are all beautiful, exactly as we are — I felt almost as ashamed of my vanity and that it took me so long to get over the shame of losing my hair. A tricky bastard, that shame. It works every angle.

Hair loss and coughing are just a couple of examples on a too-long list of things I've been ashamed of. Add to those my chimpanzee-like body hair, frequent halitosis, turned-in front teeth, and gray hair (what's left of it). Not to mention the shame I've felt about my father's gambling addiction, my brother's heroin addiction, and my own social media addiction. Then there's my shame over never wanting children and not being crazy about animals (or children) and being just a mediocre uncle at best, and a shitty one at worst. I've got some OCD going on at times, and a hearty germophobia, both of which I've deemed shameful too often to count.

No list of shame would be complete without my life's greatest shame of all: being gay. Dealing with the shame around my sexuality put all my other shames to…shame. As a gay teenager, I understood myself to be not just unusual, but vile — a sinner, an abomination, a pervert, a less-than male, a pussy, a faggot. It was a secret *never* to be revealed. I stayed closeted throughout college, only hooking up with other closeted guys when I was too drunk to stop myself, and always feeling sick and ashamed afterward. I enjoyed dating and sleeping with women, too, at the time, so though I longed for more emotional and sexual connection with men, I fulfilled some of that need with women. But it wasn't enough. It wasn't my truth.

My move to San Francisco in my twenties did more than help me get comfortable with my hair loss, however. The Bay Area broke down the door of my closet, and I finally started to accept myself. I can't and wouldn't want to imagine my sexuality any other way. But even now, at forty-five, and long after I'd grown to love myself as a gay man, I get surprised sometimes by residual gay shame. I watch myself think homophobic thoughts, or judge myself as too effeminate in moments, even though I don't believe in the idea of being too effeminate. I believe in being the most authentic version of myself, however that ends up looking and sounding. I believe in truth.

Shame, however, lives in lies. It sees beauty in standards set by magazines and movie stars and tells us we're disgusting and need to hide ourselves when we don't meet those standards (which is always). *You are ugly*, it taunts. Shame sees success as money and power and toys, and makes us feel little and worthless when we don't have enough of these things. *You are a failure*, it seethes. Shame sees our most painful experiences — betrayal, heartbreak, abuse — as reasons to blame ourselves for being hurt and as the strongest examples of how utterly flawed we are. *You are broken*, it whispers.

Shame snakes its way into all areas of our lives, telling us that how we look or what we've done or what's been done to us needs to stay a secret. Yet the real secret about shame is that it can't survive being revealed. The moment we speak of the things we're ashamed of — to a friend, to a support group, in a book (hello!) — shame's reins loosen, and its power dissipates within an air of honesty and ownership and acceptance. The truth is, we have nothing to be ashamed of, none of us. No matter how we look, or who we love, or what we've done. We've all made mistakes, we've all done wrong, and we all have reasons to ask for forgiveness. But not from a place of shame. Shame only suffocates any possible growth, any lessons we can learn from our circumstances and our actions. It doesn't allow us to acknowledge our truth. To silence shame, we must announce it. We must speak of those things about ourselves that make us sweaty and nauseous to consider, the things we spend too much energy trying to hide. Which is why I've been dreading, I mean so excited, to announce the shame I've carried about my *coughsnifflechee* (and crooked teeth, and aversion to pets, and all those other things I listed) to the world. Because what's the big deal, anyway? Nobody is perfect. But we can all do our best to be brave.

That brings me back to the airport club cougher. I sat in awe of his willingness to let his cough — a Herculean battle cry to my Pee-wee Herman croak — freely do its thing. Sure, I would've preferred he covered his mouth, but no doubt he knew his cough wasn't spreading anything. It wasn't an interloper, the effect of some contagious bug. It roared with the confidence of one who's lived in that body for years. I wonder, how long did it take to grow with such power? Was he ever self-conscious about it? If so, at what point did he finally say to himself, "Fuck it, I cough. I'm not gonna worry about what other people think." I suspect age has something to do with his nonchalance. I hope I don't give a damn what people think when I'm in my seventies. Not because that's *so* old, but because it's plenty of time to work through our insecurities. I'm forty-five, and with each year that passes, I find myself saying *fuck it* to a lot of things I worried about before. This is a good thing. My *fuck it* signifies growth.

I'm happy to say I've become more relaxed with coughing freely in public places. I know that seems like a strange goal to have, but as I can attest, there's a lot more peace in acceptance than resistance, especially of things we can't change about ourselves. As long as my cough is here, I don't think it serves me to try to deny it — not that I could.

What haven't you surrendered to? What is it about yourself you're unwilling to accept, or you're afraid others won't accept, that you're keeping secret? Can you imagine, for a moment, how different your life would be if you stopped resisting who you are and instead embraced the fullness of you — quirks, physical "imperfections," insecurities, and all? You get to decide how much power shame has in your life. You get to declare what you keep hidden, and what you express. Pick one thing you're ashamed of and share it with someone — a friend, a stranger online, your hairdresser, anyone you can trust. See how much lighter you feel, instantly, when you announce your shame. The more willing you are in sharing your entire truth, the freer you become in all areas of your life. The more often you speak of your shame, the less shame you'll have to speak of. This is a beautiful thing.

I hope one day, when my throat chakra gets balanced and my grief fully releases and Satan quits attacking me, my cough will miraculously disappear. I do believe it's possible, and I'll never lose hope in that reality, because (as I said earlier) it's seriously annoying to cough all the time. Until then, I doubt

I'll ever grow to love my *coughsnifflechee*, but I expect I'll continue to accept it more peacefully, without all the frustration and anger and shame I've felt about it for so many years. I may even become as nonchalant about my cough as my club hero was about his. One day, if I'm lucky, I may finally figure out how to be comfortably, determinedly, and gloriously shameless.

MY BROTHER

One rainy afternoon when I was ten or eleven, I grabbed my red-white-and-blue roller skates and headed to our basement to skate. I often took refuge downstairs when it was wet or cold outside, which was most of the time, in Michigan. With Donna Summer or Michael Jackson on the radio, our basement — clutter free and gigantic to a boy my age — made for a fantastic roller disco. I'd race around in circles and spin dramatically from the many support poles, pretending to compete for a medal in the Olympics. That day, I was eager to perfect my *shoot the duck*, which would've guaranteed me a gold.

As I began my descent down the stairs, I caught the eye of my older brother, Ricky. He stood with slouched shoulders, in white briefs, shackled by his wrists and ankles to a pole in the center of our basement — the very pole I used to spin around most often while I skated. My brother stood there motionless, too skinny, beside a twin mattress on the floor next to the pole. His eyes looked dark and heavy, his face pale and gaunt.

His wrists and ankles were weighted beneath metal cuffs connected to a thick chain that wrapped around the pole, giving him maybe five feet of mobility in any direction. I noticed a dirty bucket a few feet from the mattress and understood that to be his toilet. I don't remember any foul smells, but they must have been there, blocked out by the shock of seeing my brother chained up like a wild dog. Like a prisoner. Like someone who had already tried everything else to get clean.

I'm not sure if I forgot my brother was going to be taking up residence in our basement, or if my parents had neglected to mention this fact to me. That oversight seems hard to believe but was entirely possible. My parents weren't always the most adept parenters. I was the youngest of seven children, barely double digits in age, so any important bits of family drama I learned, I found out for myself through eavesdropping or reading between the lines. Or going downstairs to roller-skate. I'm confident I would've avoided the basement had I known (or even suspected) Ricky would be down there, almost naked, shitting and puking into a bucket. I wasn't *that* curious a kid. Whatever the case, there I was, and there he was, and there we were. Two brothers, one horribly uncomfortable moment.

I froze on the stairs the instant I noticed Ricky. I couldn't make sense of this incarceration, but I knew it had to do with his drug addiction. I could tell that he had agreed to this horror. He was there by his own will. When Ricky realized I was on the steps, he looked at me, stunned and ashamed, then bowed his head and diverted his eyes. We didn't speak. What was there to say? I was confused and scared to see my brother like that. I turned around, ran back up the stairs, and closed the door hard behind me. I grasped two things in that moment: Ricky was much sicker than I had realized, and my parents would do anything they could to help him get well.

Ricky was addicted to heroin. He was eighteen years older than I, and as far as anyone knew, his addiction began before I was born or when I was still an infant. I never knew him as anything but a junkie. That was the title I gave him, even before *brother*. His addiction was the lens 'hrough which I viewed him. Always high, or wanting to get high, or struggling desperately to keep from getting high. A character. An actor. Pieces of a real person, I thought, but never an honest whole. Never in control. I pitied him, and I resented him. I prayed for him, and I spited him. I loved him, and I hated him — for the brother he was, and the one he refused to be.

Ricky knew he had a problem. He didn't live in denial about his addiction, not at all. He talked openly about his inability to kick the habit. And he sought help countless times. He went to AA and NA meetings and worked with various sponsors but always went back to the needle. He checked himself into many rehabs, stayed days or weeks or months, and always went back to the needle. He even agreed to be shackled like an animal in our basement — and a second time, a couple of years later, to our parents' bed — while he endured cold-turkey withdrawals, and still he went back to the needle. Some of these attempts at going clean weren't effective at all, while others kept him out of the smack houses for a short time. Inevitably, though, his desire to get high overcame him and ran him vein-first back into his addiction.

As a kid I couldn't make sense of Ricky's addiction. I couldn't accept his inability to control himself or the notion that he was physically incapable of doing so. Along with my anger and resentment grew disgust — with the way he spoke, always with undercurrents of shame and desperation; with the way he looked, unkempt and skinny with track marks in his arms; with the way he smelled, like chemicals and city grime, a body odor that would never wash clean. More than anything, though, I grew to hate Ricky most because of the pain he caused our family, especially my parents.

I saw my father cry only twice, both times because of my brother, because of his inability to help him. I can still see my dad, laid out on our family room couch, his head in my mom's lap, his sobs filling our home. I wonder if he ever understood that nothing he or my mother did was responsible for Ricky's addiction. I wonder if any parents of an addicted child can release themselves completely from the burden of that responsibility. I've met many parents whose children have succumbed to addiction, and every single one of them continued to wonder what they could've done differently and what they had done wrong. I blamed no one but my brother for his choices, and as I saw my parents become more afraid of what would happen to him, I became angrier about what was already happening to us all.

When Ricky came by for a visit — which happened with little regularity and never with any forewarning — relief, and then tension, overcame our home. Relief that he was still alive and tension over why he had come. Because he was in trouble? To ask for money? To steal from us? We hid our valuables and locked our doors. I stuffed my piggy bank in the bottom right corner of my closet and buried it beneath a messy pile of games. We never left Ricky alone, except when he went to the bathroom, and then I wondered what he was doing in there. Was he shooting up right in our home, or was there something in there for him to steal?

My brother was an astonishingly kind and loving man, but he could not be trusted. Like many consumed by addiction, his next score was the main thing on his mind, and he'd steal from anyone — even his family — to get high. I learned this over Christmas break one year, listening in on a phone call between my parents. Ricky had broken into our home the night before and stolen all my mom's jewelry, every last piece, including the diamond watch my father had given her just days before for Christmas. The surprise on her face when she unwrapped the watch was outmatched only by the joy in my dad's smile as my mom tried it on; neither of them was particularly fancy in a diamond-watch sort of way. As my parents discussed Ricky's theft, they sounded more anguished than angry. Hopeless. Defeated. I understood then that the precautions we took when Ricky was around were necessary. And clearly not enough.

Months after my parents died, my siblings and I spent a weekend at our cottage in northern Michigan. Ricky and I stood beside the lake talking. I was fourteen at the time; he was thirty-two and had already lived nearly half his life addicted to drugs. He told me how disappointed he was that our parents died without seeing him get clean, that more than anything he wished he could take back all the agony he had caused them.

He said he would try to stay straight as a tribute to them. Even as he said these words, I think we both knew they would never become reality. I realized that my brother's efforts to get clean had more to do with loving my parents than himself, and that with my parents gone, he would likely never break free of dope. I don't believe he cared enough about himself to do so. He didn't know how.

Ricky wasn't around too much during my high school years, which usually meant he was deep into his addiction. If we weren't seeing him, he was definitely seeing the needle. My resentment and anger had started to shift, however, and continued to do so once I went away to college. I learned more about addiction and embraced the understanding of it as a disease. I believed that Ricky truly didn't have control over his behavior, that he in fact didn't have a choice in his actions. He was a victim to the drug. This belief helped me find forgiveness for the pain he caused our family. I found compassion, too, instead of only judgment.

On September 14, 1994, I came home to my apartment in San Francisco to two messages from my sister Rose. Without revealing any details, she told me to call her right away. Her voice sounded shaky, sad. I knew Ricky was dead. I had known for years I'd be receiving a call someday with news of my brother's death. It was only a matter of time. And time had run out for Ricky. Rose told me that Ricky had died early that morning from an overdose. His body had been discovered in a bathroom stall in a McDonald's somewhere in Detroit. Like the vision of my brother shackled in our basement, I knew this image would stay with me forever. And it has.

I was relieved, though, that Ricky had died. Relieved he was no longer shooting up in smack houses and fast-food joint bathrooms, or spending nights in jail. Relieved he no longer had to feel guilty and ashamed or work so hard to escape reality. I'd watched him suffer horribly my entire life, and I didn't believe he'd find a way out for himself, aside from death. The drug was too powerful, or so I thought. Now he was finally free. He had finally found peace.

My attitude about my brother, and about addiction, shifted again in the years after his death. I've had — and have — many recovering addicts for friends and recognize one critical component to a successful life in recovery, a component that wouldn't have the same power if addiction were, in fact, only an incurable disease: choice. Without choice, sobriety is impossible. And it's a constant choice, again and again, not to use. Ricky made that choice throughout his life, every single time he went to an AA meeting or checked himself into rehab or made it through a day clean. He just always chose to shoot up again. I don't know what it was about his life he couldn't find the courage to face. Even though I was his brother, I didn't know what was causing him so much pain.

I used to think heroin was more powerful than my brother, but I don't think that's the case anymore. I don't believe any drug — any addiction — is stronger than the person using, or we'd never see addicted users stop. I think Ricky was too unhappy to deal with the reality of our world as it was. He needed to create a different reality for himself, and he found a way to do it. He made his choice. Again and again. Ricky was lost but not powerless. No addict is. No person is. We all have the power to choose. Do we use, or do we abstain? If there is no choice in the habits that lead to addiction, then how can so many people choose to go beyond it? Every day, all over the world, people are moving beyond their addictions. They are choosing to free themselves.

That's not to say sobriety is an easy choice, or that alcohol and drugs aren't addictive. Of course they can be. And I don't want to in any way suggest that addicts are somehow flawed human beings if they don't get sober. Whether or not we believe those with addiction have an incurable disease or are consciously making unhealthy choices shouldn't matter in the way we talk about and treat them. Stigmatizing people who struggle with addiction certainly won't help them heal. I spent too many years looking down on my brother because of his drug problem, seeing him as broken and less than. As only a junkie. He, like all who battle addiction, was no less deserving of kindness and compassion, whatever the reason for his addiction and his inability to break free of it. There is no greater than or less than where people are concerned. We're all equal, all worthy of the same love. And aren't we all addicts to some degree? Don't we all make unhealthy choices, more often than we'd like, with the sole purpose of escaping discomfort and pain?

I've numbed myself with alcohol and drugs and sugar and sex and television and social media, all of them in excess, for periods in my life. I've never felt completely out of control in my habits (save social media), but I've certainly tasted addiction. I wasted many days chasing after empty sex online, knowing it wouldn't fulfill me but being unwilling to stop seeking it. I've downed countless pints of ice cream, as well as every dessert in existence, in failed attempts to ease my sadness. I smoked pot so regularly that I felt uneasy going to sleep without it. Addiction tempts us all. How many of us spend hours upon hours glazed over as we check our social media accounts or binge-watch TV at unhealthy levels, just to keep from having to face our real lives?

All these escapes reflect nothing more than some missing piece of happiness and connection in our lives, a deeper peace of mind that so often isn't there. It's easy to see, in this world with such anger, violence, and pain, how so many of us feel safer losing ourselves than we do finding ourselves. Escaping, rather than working to heal our realities.

I still escape sometimes, but much less often than I used to, because I always return to the same place I left behind. Don't you? And it usually feels even worse than when I left it. Whatever it is we're running from doesn't go anywhere. It may not chase us every second, but it won't disappear, either. The truth remains. Which is why drug addicts and alcoholics — and frankly, many of us — don't like to be sober, consciously aware of ourselves and the planet. The whole truth lives in sobriety, and the whole truth is never pretty for any of us. It can, however, be tolerable. It can become something we're able to live with, even accept and honor, without needing to numb ourselves to do so. With our willingness, and with support.

Rather than turn to alcohol, drugs, gambling, or food when we feel sad or lonely, what if we just allowed ourselves to feel sad and lonely? Like human beings feel sometimes. When did it become destructive to feel anything but happy? Nobody is always happy. Maybe you're scared? I know I am. The world is a scary place, and it makes perfect sense to be scared at times. Anyone paying attention feels scared, and angry, and sad, and overwhelmed in moments. Maybe often. Those of us with traumatic childhoods don't just grow into adulthood forgetting our pasts. The trauma comes with us, and either we figure out a way to face and accept it or we make a choice to escape it. We numb ourselves from its effects. It's no wonder numerous studies link childhood trauma to susceptibility to addiction.

I used to be so afraid to be with my sadness — over my parents' death, my brother's addiction, the state of the world — that I did everything in my power to avoid it. I turned my sadness into a monster that would crush me if I faced it. So I didn't. Only when I started to look at my sadness honestly, to sit in it and feel the pain of it, was I able to see that I could survive it. It wasn't comfortable, but it didn't destroy me; it made me stronger and more compassionate, for myself and others. I don't fear my sadness like I used to. Or my anger, or my pain. I pay attention to them, I feel them, I stay as open as I can to the lessons they want me to learn. And I take care of and love myself through them. Love matters. It's our greatest healer.

The more I focus on love, the more able I am to accept my whole truth and the whole truth of others. Love reminds me I have nothing to be ashamed of and therefore don't need to numb myself out of shame. Love encourages me to find forgiveness so that I don't have to escape my anger and blame. Love pushes me to seek connection so that I am no longer compelled to be destructive in my loneliness. Love insists

I am worthy, just as I am, and that I am strong enough to accept and love myself, without needing to mask my truth. Every single time we choose love, we're choosing our health and well-being. And the more we choose love, the more likely we are to create for ourselves the kind of lives we won't need to escape from.

I was resigned to Ricky's imminent overdose, because I believed he was weak and could never overcome his addiction. I was so wrong. I now know he could have. As long as you're breathing, and you want it, recovery is always possible. For addicts, and for all of us. Miracles happen *all the time*. We have no idea what the future holds or what one choice will set us on a completely different path. What one choice will stop us from numbing. I'm sorry I never got to see my brother make that one choice. I would have loved to watch him fly free.

I labeled Ricky a junkie while he was alive, and he was so much more. He was as kindhearted a man as I've ever known, with a giant smile he offered willingly to everyone who crossed his path. When I picture him now, it's almost always with that smile stamped on his face, his loving blue eyes open for connection. He was funny and charming and felt comfortable talking to anyone, about anything. An instant friend. He was gentle, so gentle, ultimately too gentle for this reality. He loved our family with his whole heart but was never able to find a true home in our world.

I still sometimes think of Ricky in the basement, in his underwear, shackled to that pole. I can see the chains, and the mattress, and the bucket. I can feel his shame. The memory has haunted me. But only because I wasn't able to see in him what I'm able to see now — a man willing to stand in his pain without an escape, a man willing to trust his parents to guide him through hell, a man willing to do anything to heal himself. What's braver than that?

I love my brother, even more in his death than I did when he was alive. My love for him is no longer muddied with anger or judgment or blame or anything other than the pure acceptance of who he was and what he had to offer while he was here. Which was, above everything else, his big love for us all.

TEA TIME

just made myself a perfect cup of green tea. Steeped for one minute and forty-five seconds. In hot, but not boiling, water. A floral scent, with a hint of hazelnut, exactly as I like it. I just took a sip, in fact, and it's delicious, like liquid, tasty grass or hot vegetable water — but good. My friend Melanie says green tea tastes like worms wrapped in fish. I don't know where she's been eating, but I think green tea tastes like the earth, just not as dirty.

I used to drink green tea nearly every day. I still love it, and I drink it occasionally, but I traded in the subtle antioxidant lift of the bagged tea leaves for the more body-quaking buzz of the arabica bean. That's a dramatic way of saying I drink coffee now. Usually a cup in the afternoon, with — are you ready for this — a coconut-almond-chia-milk blend or, on occasion, a touch of Baileys. Yum. Baileys, you may not know, also makes for a delicious addition to oatmeal. I learned this at a B&B in Ireland that served their oatmeal (I mean, porridge) with Baileys instead of milk. Not surprisingly, it was the best oatmeal/porridge I'd ever had and the only time a bowl of oats had me buzzing.

I eat a lot of oatmeal and could write about it for pages, but that would almost certainly prevent you from finishing this chapter. So let's get back to my green tea, because nothing says page-turner like tea.

Green tea shouldn't steep for too long. One to three minutes, max. After much experimentation, I've found one minute and forty-five seconds to be my ideal flavor zone. Anything more than three minutes enters "what the hell is this?" territory. The longer it steeps, the more bitter it tastes. At five minutes, you're basically drinking overcooked, overripe broccoli water. At six minutes, a dirty ashtray. After that, scorched earth. You may as well just burn a piece of toast beyond recognition and then lick it over and over again.

For years, when I would make myself a cup of green tea, I'd pour the hot water over my tea bag, look at the clock (on my phone, typically), and then, with intention, say to myself, "Remember the tea. Remember the tea. Remember the tea." Always three times, for whatever reason. Ritual is ritual. We remember things when we repeat them to ourselves, right? Wrong. Probably 80 percent of the time, I'd forget about the tea. I'd rush back into the kitchen many minutes later, hopeful I hadn't ruined another cup but certain I had. I'd take a hesitant sip, only to be assaulted by the taste of cat urine. Yes, after ten minutes of steeping, it goes all-out cat piss. This is just a guess, of course, as I've never tasted cat pee. I have, however, had several of my possessions pissed on by one of my sister's cats, who had emotional problems. Really, the cat saw a psychologist, which may have boosted the cat's overall happiness, but it didn't stop her from peeing in my shoes.

Let's get back to green tea.

So, my oversteeped tea often ended up tasting like what I imagine cat piss to taste like. (Not an issue when you're drinking chamomile tea, by the way — that flower can steep forever.) I'm not sure what to blame — my deep commitment to laziness or not wanting to waste what had been a perfectly good tea bag — but I'd drink the terrible tea. Every time. I'd grimace through sip after sip, like taking shots of 100 proof moonshine.

Bottom line: I've sucked down more shitty cups of green tea than good ones.

It didn't have to be that way. An obvious solution existed for my green tea woes: use a timer. Duh. That would have required not just picking up my cell phone to check the time but also taking fifteen extra seconds to set the timer. Who's got fifteen seconds to spare when you're doing absolutely nothing? I decided, after years of imbibing mostly bad tea, that *I* did indeed have fifteen seconds to spare, and that I would trade in my stunning laziness for basic self-care.

Sound the trumpets...I started timing my green tea.

I poured the hot (never boiling) water over the bag, set the timer for 1:45, and checked Facebook or washed dishes or did who knows what for 105 seconds until the quacking duck alarm on my phone told me my tea was ready. Day after day, the ducks quacked, and day after day, I enjoyed a perfect cup of green tea, which, as you might suspect, tastes much better than a dirty ashtray or hot cat urine, except perhaps to my friend Melanie, who may prefer those to worms rolled in fish. I don't know, you'd have to ask her.

At this point in the story, or perhaps even before this point, you may be wondering why the hell you're reading this book and what a man who chose to drink nasty-ass tea for years instead of simply setting a timer could possibly have to teach you. I understand your concern. We'll get there, but let's talk about my underwear first.

One day, as I sat writing at my desk (a.k.a. the kitchen table), enjoying a positively perfect cup of green tea (much like right now), I noticed myself squirming around in the chair, repeatedly dislodging my underwear from my butt crack. I sat there for a couple of hours — writing, squirming, dislodging, writing, squirming, dislodging — giving as much thought to my underwear as I was to my writing.

I hate these underwear.

These underwear suck.

Why are they so uncomfortable?

Then it occurred to me — sound the trumpets again: I didn't have to wear those underwear. Duh. I could in fact remove them from my body and rid myself of the discomfort that I'd been experiencing all morning. Double-duh. That's what I did. I had never liked that pair of underwear. They were a literal pain in my ass. You know the type. Always shifting and riding, never comfortable, no matter what you do. We all have underwear we hate. Even crazier, we all keep wearing underwear we hate. I didn't just take them off, either. I grabbed a pair of scissors and cut them to pieces, a firm declaration of my freedom from their britches. (I did wash the scissors afterward, in case you were wondering. I open my oatmeal packs with those.)

From there, I marched into my bedroom and over to the dresser. I pulled out my underwear drawer with the focus of a surgeon and extracted two other malignant pairs I've never liked — the gray Calvin Kleins that have always crushed my package (I don't like the word *package*, either, but what would you call genitalia in a book like this?) and the white 2(X)ISTs that have stretched out like bloomers and are far better suited for the eighty-year-old version of myself — the one who splashes Baileys in his oatmeal every single morning. Plus, let's be honest, white is not a good color choice for underwear. I think anyone who's ever done laundry would agree. I'd rather be blissfully unaware of the track marks hidden in my black undies, and extra blissfully unaware of the track marks left in my partner's. White briefs invite unfortunate surprises.

Now we've done it. We've devolved from cat piss to track marks. I had no idea this would happen, I swear. But here we are. Let's make the most of it.

I didn't get all dramatic and cut up the other two pairs of underwear. They hadn't been tormenting me all morning and didn't deserve such harsh punishment. I just threw them out, on top of the sliced-up remnants of the other pair, and I felt good, as someone feels when he's taking care of himself.

And that's the point (at last, thank God; I bet you never thought it would happen): self-care matters.

Self-care is having its moment. Not a day goes by that I don't see articles, blog posts and, of course, memes about self-care, of smiling people in bathtubs, on walks in nature, or, coincidentally, sipping mugs of what I assume to be some healthy tea but, based on the crazy, blissed-out look in their eyes, may in fact be quadruple espressos. People everywhere are trying to take better care of themselves. This is great. Important. Necessary. No one will be able to take care of you better than you're able to take care of you, if you choose to do it. Also, no one stands to benefit more from your self-care than you.

Self-care tends to lead to greater happiness, or at least more frequent bouts of it. Unlike happiness, however, which is a feeling and not a choice, self-care mandates choosing, again and again, to be good to ourselves. We hold the power to improve our lives by making choices that serve our well-being.

Yes, self-care is selfish. Don't let that stop you. Selfish isn't always a bad thing. Most things are selfish, anyway. We tend to make choices in order to feel better in some way or to keep from feeling worse. Most selflessness comes with some selfishness wrapped into it. We almost always consider ourselves in the choices we make, even when we think we're only considering others. It feels pretty great to selflessly consider others, doesn't it? The beauty of selfish self-care is that by taking care of ourselves, we're serving not only ourselves but also everyone who comes in contact with us. I'm much more pleasant to be around after a shower, or a long nap, or holding a warm cup of perfectly steeped green tea whilst wearing well-fitted underwear. (That will likely be the only time you see the word *whilst* in this book, so I hope you enjoyed it.)

Once I began to time my tea, I quickly gave up my timerless ways. Perfect cup of tea after perfect cup of tea changes a man. Now I don't even think to make a cup of green tea without setting the timer on my phone. It's become a part of the process, built into the ritual. Self-care as habit. I also don't wear uncomfortable underwear anymore, except for a pair of black Jockeys that still ride up my crack occasionally but look too good to part with. We all make our compromises. When we take an honest look at our lives, however, we're likely to find we don't have to compromise our self-care as much as we've been doing.

We can do things differently.

Every time I chose to make and drink a cup of cat-piss tea, I disrespected myself as unworthy of my time and care. Every hour I spent in crack-attack underwear equaled sixty minutes of self-abuse. That's not hyperbole. If we're not making choices that reflect self-care, we're likely making choices that don't. We're saying, energetically, that we don't matter enough to take care of ourselves. We don't love ourselves enough. Maybe that's true for you. I know it's been true for me. Still is, sometimes. We can find our way to self-love, however, through relentless self-care. That's just one of many paths, so drench yourself in scented baths. (That will likely be the only intentional rhyme in this book, but no promises.)

The more we take care of ourselves, the more natural it becomes. Like nose-picking or binge-watching TV shows, we find ourselves doing it without even thinking about it. Timed green tea leads to scissored underwear leads to ten quiet minutes on the balcony to start each day. These choices matter. We also become more aware of those moments when we're not caring for ourselves, moments that before may have felt natural but now feel unhealthy or unwelcome. Really, how long are you going to use that ratty old toothbrush that scratches your gums? (That's a question for me, FYI.)

Little tweaks go a long way.

Though inexplicably it took me years to do it, timing my tea counts as an easy fix. So does tossing out my uncomfortable underwear. Where are your easy fixes? Isn't it time to make some of them? Think of all the ways you could make simple tweaks to take better care of yourself. Are you still wearing those shoes that give you blisters or those jeans that barely button and leave a gnarly imprint around your waist when you take them off? Are you drinking enough water? Getting enough sleep? And what about that underwear drawer? Is it time to grab the scissors? We don't have to be resigned to discomfort, not when more comfortable options await us.

Self-care means setting boundaries with others as well. As we grow more adept at taking care of ourselves, we become clearer about our needs and about the things that feel, and don't feel, okay with us. Speak them. If it's not okay for strangers to rub your bald head like it's a magic eight ball, say it. (Sorry, that example may be a touch specific to me.) If your friend's teasing feels more hurtful than funny, tell her. If you need more alone time in your relationship, let your partner know. Sure, some people may judge your clarity as difficult or unfriendly, but the majority will appreciate knowing what works for you. Most of us don't take joy in overstepping each other's boundaries; we often don't even know we're doing it. We foster healthier, more honest relationships with others, and in turn take better care of ourselves, when we're willing to communicate our boundaries clearly. With clear boundaries, we can bypass the resentment that comes with feeling taken for granted and get down to the important business of loving.

Love is our most important business, and any love we give ourselves is love that serves us all. Selfishness, supported by love, acts as a healer, too.

In the spirit of taking care of myself, I just took a short break to watch one of my favorite videos — sixteen seconds of a puppy sitting upright at a table, lapping up a green smoothie. I watched it six or seven times in a row, laughing wildly, marveling at the puppy's poise, and also at the size of his green-stained tongue, which would look more appropriate on a baby giraffe than that furry little lapdog. I'm sitting here in comfortable underwear, having just taken the last sip of my perfect cup of green tea and, now, because I've finished this chapter and want some fresh air, I'm gonna go for a walk.

Peace comes in bits and pieces, in intentional habits, in the choices we make that support the belief that we're worthy, and in the moments we decide, no matter what, to take care of ourselves. And then we do.

FLOP

I peed my pants in second grade. On Valentine's Day. Just after lunch in Mrs. Brown's class. She was strict, and I was afraid to ask her for a bathroom pass, because, "You could have gone during lunch." So I tried to hold it, until I couldn't. Luckily, I was the class mailman that week, so I walked to the back corner of our classroom and filed Valentine's Day cards into everyone's mail slots. As Mrs. Brown talked basic mathematics, I peed my pants. What relief! Warm and immediate. My classmates sat at their desks, oblivious to the wet stain on my pants and the yellow puddle on the floor. I hurried back to my desk without anyone realizing what I'd done.

Success!

Ten minutes later, however, Jenny Stein, the clever girl I had a crush on, yelled from the mailboxes, "There's water all over the floor, and it looks kind of yellow."

Uh-oh.

I slunk at my desk, in my soaked pants, terrified I'd be found out. Mrs. Brown looked at me with knowing eyes but said nothing. A gift I'll never forget. None of the kids ever knew I pissed myself. Had they found out, they would have never let me forget it. *Scotty Potty*, all the way through high school.

A few years ago, decades after narrowly escaping that Scotty Potty fate, a very public failure carried me back to that Valentine's Day. Only in this version, I crapped my pants in the middle of the classroom, and everybody watched. In this version, no kind soul helped hide my secret — it was out there for all the world to see.

●　●　●

It started out as a dream come true. A big dream, too. I wrote a screenplay that got produced and released as a feature film in 2012. Released nationwide, that is, on more than two thousand movie screens across the United States. That's what the film industry calls a very wide release, an especially unusual feat for an independent film like ours. Even *Pulp Fiction* made it to fewer than fifteen hundred screens. Take that, Quentin Tarantino. Yeah, I was feeling pretty good, like an up-and-coming Hollywood screenwriter. Like a guy on his way to making it. It was just a matter of time before I got my star on Hollywood Blvd.

A dream come true.

Until the nightmare began.

Said film — *The Oogieloves in the Big Balloon Adventure* — an interactive children's musical, bombed critically and commercially. Extraordinarily so. Referred to by critics as a *train wreck, cloyingly unbearable,* and *akin to witnessing the end of the world,* the film found no love with audiences, either. It went on to become the lowest-grossing wide-release film *in history.* As in *ever.* It still holds that unenviable title, which makes me, still, the unenviable titleholder: writer of the lowest-grossing wide-release film *in history,* as in *ever.*

I feared I would forever go down as the guy who wrote the biggest flop of all time. A laughingstock. My potential screen-writing career would disintegrate. People would point and snicker at me in restaurants, and industry folk would fake-cough "loser" in my presence. My friends would secretly pity me, and some would be embarrassed to hang out with me, lest the truth of my script came out at dinner parties. I could become president, or find the cure for cancer, and I would still be the dude who wrote that disastrous Oogieloves movie. Cue the snark. Of course, the film was so unsuccessful that most people still don't know it even existed, and even fewer have any clue who I am. And, a cure for cancer obviously outshines any box office disaster. Our minds are masters of worst-case scenarios, though, and my mind locked onto a future of over-whelming humiliation.

My sister, in a genuine attempt to comfort me when it became clear the film had epically bombed, proclaimed, "Your movie will probably be an answer on *Jeopardy* someday!" *Thanks, sis.* As far as I'm aware, no answer from Alex Trebek has elicited the question, "What are...the Oogieloves?" Though I think that's what moviegoers themselves were won-dering, both the few who saw the film and the many who avoided it. I still have trouble accurately answering that question: giant, lovable, freaky puppet-like creatures that exclaim a lot?

The film opened on August 29, 2012. *Oogust* 29, according to the posters. I spent the day with a friend at the US Open tennis tournament, unsuccessfully trying to keep my mind off the film's first day. A solid opening weekend would have guaranteed many years of Oogieloves income — from ticket sales, merchandising, and sequels, two of which I had already written and would only be produced if the first film did well. The Oogieloves were not only going to entertain children for years to come; they were going to earn me a shit-ton of cash in doing so. That was the hope, anyway. Life had a different plan in store.

Many of us gathered at the producer's apartment that evening, to celebrate what we hoped would be a successful opening. None of us expected blockbuster numbers, but we couldn't have predicted the degree to which the film would flop. When the box office receipts started to trickle in, they made it clear the movie had bombed. We're talking nuclear. Several of the screens reported zero admissions. As in no one bought a single ticket. Have you ever been alone in a movie theater? If so, you would have been one person more than my film had in some of its theaters. The celebration quickly turned into a wake, as we all mourned, among other things, our reputations and whatever futures we had tied to the success of the film.

The disappointment and embarrassment hit instantly and profoundly, like realizing you had thrown out a multimillion-dollar lottery ticket *and* discovering the entire country had

seen video footage of you making love to a burrito. I think I
went into shock. I had no control over the fate of the film, yet
its fate had immediately and irrevocably squashed my dignity,
and my writing career. Or so I thought. My partner, Goran
(G), took one look at me and called in sick to work for the rest
of the week.

I can laugh about the bruising experience now and write
this lighthearted chapter about my most public failure, but not
before feeling the pain of it. Not before questioning my worth,
as a creative and a human being. I tried to ignore the barrage of criticism and attempted to remind myself that other
people's opinions in no way define me. But it stung. All of it.
Every negative review, every mean tweet, every uncomfortable
conversation with friends who had seen the film and stuttered
through some awkward version of "good job" or "congratula-
tions." I knew better than to ask, "What did you think of it?"

I felt like a fraud, a hack who had no business believing
he could write anything, let alone movies. Like a disappointment, to the production team and investors who had put
their faith in me, to my family and friends who had rooted
for me, and to G, who had been by my side throughout and
who, like me, had seen the potential success of the film as a
means to a financial security neither of us had ever known. I
felt like a joke. Worse, a punch line. Even though the script is
just one component of a film, I took all the negative criticism
personally.

The film failed.

Therefore I failed.

Therefore I was a failure.

I fell into a depression for a couple of weeks. The sting lasted much longer, but the shock and despair subsided. I ached for the entire cast and crew that had worked so hard on the film, only to see it ridiculed mercilessly. The film's failure brought out even more bullies, all salivating at the opportunity to punish it, and the team behind it even further. Criticism gave way to cruelty; kindness fell to cynicism. I responded to the backlash with an essay I posted on my Facebook page. In it, I wrote, "You'd think we were trying to turn three-year-olds on to the crack pipe." I understood hating the movie, but I couldn't make sense of the venom. One hater suggested the creatives behind the film should be beaten to death. Needless to say, comments like that only strengthened my feelings of failure.

● ● ●

Not everyone has an Oogieloves, but we all know failure. It's never fun to fail, at anything. Have you ever been fired from a job or not hired after an interview? Dieted to lose weight, only to put more back on? Gone on a terrific first date and then gotten rejected before the second one happened? We face variations of failure constantly. Many of us have quit smoking and started up again a few weeks later. We've missed our kids' sporting events. We've gotten another parking ticket we can't comfortably afford to pay. We've overslept and arrived late to a meeting. We've burned dinner. We've undercooked breakfast.

Fail. Fail. Fail.

It sucks when we don't show up for ourselves, or others,

the way we want to. Our minds want us to feel ashamed when we fail, so that we stop taking risks and we stay safe in our comfort zones. My mind has used my failures to convince me I am incapable or unworthy or untalented. "You will fail again," it tells me, "and it will hurt even more next time." Yes, it's painful to fail, and it's important to feel our feelings, including the disappointment and sadness that often accompany failure. I have yet to heal any aspect of my life through denial. Still, it's just as important to recognize that our failures don't define us. You are not your burned dinner, or your smoking habit. I am not the Oogieloves. I wrote a box office bomb. So what? That in no way speaks to the quality of my character. I continued to write and share my creativity with the world, even after failing extravagantly. Now *that* says something about me.

Most successes arise from a mountain of failures, each one unpredictable and scary. We all fear failure, but that doesn't have to stop us from working toward success. When we honestly acknowledge our failures and learn from them what we can, we create a path to move forward, and to succeed. We can live our lives determined to avoid failure, but in doing so we're certain to avoid taking chances that might transform our lives in myriad positive ways. We're also certain to prevent ourselves from learning how to handle failure when we inevitably encounter it. Sure, we fail less by not trying much, but we succeed less, too.

Of course, when we take an honest look at our definition of success, we may discover we're finding it more often than we realize. How do you define success? I have too often gauged success by how people responded to whatever I created or achieved, without taking the time to honor the process of creation. I've invited disappointment by attaching myself to factors beyond my control. Because the Oogieloves failed both critically and commercially, I believed I failed as a writer. Was it not a success that I completed the script? Or that the screenplay was produced into a film? Or that the film defied every odd in Hollywood and made it into theaters? I bought into the idea that the film failed because it bombed. But what about the journey to get to opening day? It's so rarely the outcome that speaks to who we are and what we've achieved. What matters most are the steps we take to reach that outcome.

I had a blast writing the Oogieloves. I spent nights lost in silliness, thinking up visionary lyrics like "Wobble with your wiggle, with your wiggle wobble too" and "If you want a milkshake, you know what to do. March and moo!" I danced around my bedroom as I imagined Goobie, Zoozie, and Toofie (the actual Oogieloves) romping through LovelyLoveVille in search of magical balloons for their dear friend Schluufy the Pillow's surprise party. (Don't worry, none of that should make any sense to you.) I sang the songs to G, until, like me, he couldn't get them out of his head. He's still cursing me for "Pineapple upside-down flapjacks, clap clap jack, for the flapjacks." I'm still cursing myself for that one, too. It really sticks after the five hundredth listen.

Writing the script brought me joy. And as a guy with folders of incomplete writing projects, finishing the script felt terrific. Like success.

If the standard definition of *failure* is "lack of success," let's consider how we define success before we deem ourselves a failure.

Even though I don't define success in terms of money, power, and popularity, I see how my mind still gets lost in those false notions of what it means to be successful. My ego wants more cash, more cachet, and more clicks. There can't ever be enough of any of them. That's not success, of course. That's conditioning. Addiction. Desperation.

Love invites me to see success differently, as the fullest embodiment of kindness and compassion I'm capable of expressing. When I'm loving, I'm successful. When I'm forgiving, I'm successful, too. I've come to view success through a lens of humanity, and the degree to which I'm successful directly aligns with the degree to which I love myself and my fellow human beings. This definition of success fires me up and keeps me striving for more.

I still fail constantly, especially in the arena of personal development. Every time I act cruelly, I fail at being kind. Every time I snap at my partner, I fail at being patient. Every time I condemn someone for her choices, I fail at being accepting. If for me success equals my capacity for love, then it's incumbent on me to be aware when I fail to find love so that I can succeed in returning to it. Yes, I'm failing all the time, but I'm succeeding even more often. When I smile at a stranger, I'm succeeding at kindness. Connecting with another's pain is a success at compassion. All moments of forgiveness and authenticity and vulnerability reflect a commitment to love and are therefore successes, too.

I still get turned on by money, power, and popularity,

by the way, much more often than I'd like, but accepting rather than denying the reality of those desires also serves my growth. Just as transcending those desires does. I hope one day to wholly embody what I understand to be true — that neither money nor power nor popularity ultimately has anything to do with a life of meaning or joy. Love is where I find my deepest meaning and my greatest joy. Love is what drives me to express myself the most authentically, and to connect with others the most openly, more than money, power, and popularity ever could.

● ● ●

When I think of the Oogieloves now, a strange pride overcomes me. *I* wrote the Oogieloves, the biggest flop of all time. Li'l ol' me. No one else can say that. (I realize it's likely no one else wishes they could say that.) I've got conversation fodder till the day I die. Not to mention a much thicker skin, and a chapter in this book. There's also a certain freedom that comes with writing the biggest bomb ever: you can't sink lower than rock bottom. So often we keep ourselves from making brave choices because we don't want to relive the pain or embarrassment of the terrible thing that happened to us before. We don't want to relive the Oogieloves. But it rarely gets worse than the event that has us so scared to begin with. I've already written the lowest-grossing wide-release film in history. Am I really in danger of topping that? If I did, I'd survive. And I'd keep writing.

That's all we can ever do in the face of failure: just keep doing.

Before starting this chapter, I reread some of the more scathing Oogieloves reviews, which included descriptions like *excruciating* and *ultimately oppressive*. I scrolled through pages of Twitter comments, nearly all of which ridiculed the film. *If you plop your kid in front of Oogieloves you are an awful parent.* I listened to one of the many anti-Oogieloves podcast episodes out there, during which one host suggested the movie *was designed to play for prisoners of war while you're interrogating them.* I laughed as I read and listened to the mockery and insults. Then my strange pride disintegrated as my insides heated up, and I broke out into a full-body sweat. Head to toe. I felt horribly judged and embarrassed all over again. Like Scotty Potty, only the pants-crapping version.

And it passed, as feelings always do.

I remembered how one of the PR guys for the film suggested I launch my own Facebook page to announce myself as the film's writer, to promote the film before its release, and to engage with potential fans. I took his advice and started my author page on Facebook. I did a little prerelease promotion but ultimately didn't engage with a lot of Oogieloves fans, mostly because there weren't that many.

After the film flopped, I still had my Facebook page and some time to consider what I wanted to do with it. I started to write posts about the things that mattered most to me, such as kindness, authenticity, compassion, and love. People began to notice my page and share my posts. In a few years, a few hundred thousand were following it, and my posts were reaching millions of people every week. It's in great part due to the success of my Facebook page that this book even exists. And without the failure of the Oogieloves, my Facebook page may never have existed.

We have no idea what seeds we're planting as we create our lives, or if and when they'll be sown. All we can do is continue to create, despite the threat or reality of failure, and be aware and grateful when our courage has made way for a harvest.

I'VE BEEN THERE, HONEY

I sat down for my flight to Los Angeles and noticed, even before buckling up, that the woman sitting across the aisle from me seemed upset. She stared at the seat in front of her, eyes glazed over with sadness, and clutched a crumpled Kleenex with which she dabbed at her eyes and nose repeatedly. She had either just finished crying or was about to start. Perhaps both.

I wanted to hug her.

The aisle emptied of passengers making their way to their seats, and I glanced again at the woman, pulled in by her sadness. I considered handing her a fresh tissue or asking her if she was okay, even though I knew she wasn't. Anything to let her know she wasn't alone. But I've cried on planes more times than I can count, for any number of reasons (usually the movie), and the last thing I would've wanted was for someone to try to talk with me through my tears. I decided it was best, right then, to give her some space, so I didn't say anything.

While I was deliberating what to do, one of the flight attendants — a bright-eyed African-American woman with thick blonde braids and a giant smile — spotted the woman and walked right up to her. She saw someone in pain and responded instinctively.

"Honey, what's wrong?" she asked the woman, who was at least fifteen years her senior.

The woman hesitated, her eyes welling up. "My father died last week," she replied, choked up. I assumed she was on her way to or from his funeral.

The flight attendant bent over, grabbed the woman's hand, looked her right in the eyes, and said, "I've been there, honey. I've been there." She opened her arms, and the woman leaned into them, her tears falling freely then. The flight attendant held on to her, and there they stayed for many seconds, two strangers intimately connected by their shared experience of having lost a father. Two human beings not just seeing but feeling each other.

The flight attendant released the woman from the hug but held both her hands tightly. "I'm gonna be checking on you all the time, but you speak up if you need anything at all, okay?"

The woman nodded.

"Anything, I mean it," the flight attendant said.

"Thank you, sweetheart," the woman replied.

The flight attendant walked to the front of the plane to prepare for takeoff, and the crying woman closed her eyes and tilted her head ever so slightly downward. As if in prayer.

●　●　●

There's a huge difference between sympathy and empathy, between "I'm sorry" and "I've been there." It's not that sympathy is bad. It's just that empathy invites a connection that sympathy simply can't. Sympathy says, "I feel sorry for you," while empathy declares, "I am you." Sympathy encourages us to find compassion, from a distance, for another's misfortune. Empathy demands that we revisit our own pain in order to relate to someone else's. Sympathy requires our kindness. Empathy requires our vulnerability.

The flight attendant made it clear to the woman that she wasn't alone in her loss. "I've been there, honey" removed any separation that "I'm so sorry, honey" might have created. I suspect the crying woman felt understood rather than just pitied for her grief. The difference was profound.

My friend Jess called to tell me she had been fired from her job. She raged about how mistreated she felt by her boss, cried over how embarrassed she felt for having been let go in such a dismissive way, and then panicked from the fear of not knowing how she would support herself. Yes, I told her I was sorry she'd been fired, but I also let her know I understood, and that I had been fired once and felt all those things, too — rage, sadness, and panic. I had been there, and I knew how much it sucked. I rested in my own experience to make myself more available to hers. I did my best to listen, empathetically, without judgment, and without needing to fix anything. I told her I loved and believed in her and reminded her that, in time, we fired people rose like phoenixes to greater heights. Jess was still bummed about getting fired, but I know she felt supported and much less alone in her frustration.

Empathy helps.

Consider situations in which it helped immensely to know that others could relate to what you were going through. After a brutal breakup, we don't want someone who's never had their heart broken telling us to get over it. We want to sob to a friend who knows the grief of a broken heart and the time it can take to move on. If you're a parent being driven crazy by your toddler, you may not seek out your single friends to commiserate, not when you've got other struggling parent friends who really get what you're going through. It's comforting to be heard; it's empowering to be understood.

Human beings don't long just for connection; we long for empathetic connection.

When we can relate to someone going through a difficult time, when we can empathize with her struggle, we serve her by letting her know. I've spoken with thousands of people over the years about my parents' murder, almost always to a reaction of shock, and then sympathy. I've cried into the arms of close friends who would've sold their souls to take away my pain. Their compassion and love touched me deeply, of course, and I'm grateful to have had so many loved ones with whom I could unravel. But something entirely different happens when I encounter others who lost their parents when they were young. Others who understand what it's like to live most of their lives without a mom and dad, or who know the pain of losing a loved one to murder. Others who have been there. In our shared experience, we can offer each other the distinct — divine — comfort of empathy. This is how we help each other feel less alone in our individual struggles.

Empathy eliminates separation. It fosters connection. I was my friend Jess. The flight attendant was the grieving woman. That's the thing about being human — we are all each other. Even when we can't relate to the exact same situation as another, we can still make an effort to empathize. We have probably lived some version of being there. Heartache is heartache, after all. Anger is anger. Grief is grief. We have all walked the path between joy and sorrow, stopping at every emotion along the way. Empathy asks us to be willing to share ourselves with each other, willing to be vulnerable and speak about our pain so that others feel the freedom to speak about theirs.

Empathy is a gift, to give and to receive.

One of the things I love most about my Facebook community is our willingness to empathize with each other's experiences. When people post about depression, addiction, chronic pain, grief, anxiety, or whatever else, others respond with comments that make it clear to those who shared that they are not alone. They have been there, too. The point is not to hijack someone else's experience, or to drone on about our own struggles, but to respond in a way that lets others know they're not mutants for feeling the way they feel. Likely, many of us have experienced whatever they're experiencing, or something very similar.

I think about my relationship and the many times I've been frustrated with my partner, G, simply because I didn't take the time to consider — and honor — his experience. He's slow to make big changes, which provokes my impatience. I dive into change, which undermines his sense of stability. He likes background noise in our home, because it makes him feel more comfortable. I like silence, because it helps me relax. We each have our reasons for our preferences and choices. Although it may feel like it at times, we're not actively working to annoy each other. Still, too often I've chosen judgment over empathy. Rather than putting myself in his shoes, or connecting to a time when I've felt something similar, I've just decided he was wrong. *He should be more sensitive*, I think, or, *he is doing that on purpose*. All relationships require negotiation, of course, and the compromise conversations flow much more smoothly when empathy is involved. They're almost certain to flounder without it.

We don't need empathy just in our intimate relationships, either. All healthy connections call for it. Just think about our crazy planet. So much of the disconnection we see in our world, so much of the division and anger that exist between human beings, could be alleviated by a more conscious attempt — by all of us — to be more empathetic. We're all judging and screaming at each other about how wrong everyone else is and how right we are, without really taking the time to consider each other's experience. How much more peaceful would our world be if we stopped to imagine what it's like to walk in each other's shoes? Or if we simply acknowledged it when we already have? Without judgment or having to agree with a person's choices, and without needing to have experienced whatever it is they're going through, we can always choose to empathize. We can declare, "I've been there" or that we're doing our best to imagine what it's like to be there.

Empathy is a conscious choice and, like all conscious choices, it takes practice. The more we do it, the better we become at it — until empathy, rather than just sympathy, is our go-to response.

The next time you're inclined to sympathize, see if there's an opportunity to empathize. Call on your courage, take that person's hand, look him in the eyes, and let him know you've been there. Those are the types of connections that change people, that foster love, that remind us we are all brothers and sisters. Ultimately, we *are* all brothers and sisters. And in some way, we have all been there, honey.

As I sat on that LA-bound flight, I imagined moving to the empty seat beside the crying woman and gently holding her hand through the journey, letting her know I felt her pain and that she was not alone. I also imagined hugging the flight attendant and telling her what an extraordinary human being she was and then writing a pages-long letter to the airline detailing the pure grace with which she had engaged the woman across the aisle.

I didn't do any of those things.

When we landed, I did help the woman get her bag down from the overhead bin. "You're a sweetheart," she told me.

As we deplaned, I watched the flight attendant give the woman a huge hug. The woman squeezed the flight attendant's hand one last time before she stepped off the plane.

As I walked up, the flight attendant smiled at me, a lightning bolt of kindness. "You enjoy LA. Thank you for flying with us today!"

"Thank *you* for everything," I replied. She couldn't have known I was referring to so much more than the peanuts and pretzels she had given me.

THE MELTDOWN

My partner, G, and I have lived in Panama City, Panama, for the past three years. G is a commercial airline pilot and got a job offer from Copa, Panama's main airline. We were living in Brooklyn at the time, and though we liked our loft apartment, loved our view of the Manhattan skyline, and obsessed over the food in our Williamsburg/Greenpoint neighborhood, we had grown sick of the busy, dirty, noisy city. We wanted a change and both felt drawn to the idea of an adventure abroad. So we moved to Panama City — a not-so-busy but still dirty and noisy city. A suffocatingly hot and humid city. A city of mediocre and overpriced food. Did I mention the heat? Damn, it's hot here.

At least we're abroad. And we have another killer view.

Neither G nor I have fallen in love with the city (or even fallen in like). We're moving back to the States very soon, in fact. Though we've made a handful of close friends here, really like our apartment, and have even found some restaurants we love, we ultimately haven't vibed with the place. I've struggled with being here a bit more than G, in part because he escapes a lot for work, and in part because I'm higher maintenance than he is. (I will never admit this to him, of course.) I've felt lonely and isolated, frustrated by my inability to learn Spanish well, and I've often longed to live somewhere else. (Sorry, Panama, it's not you, it's me.) Our move here has always been temporary, and that fact, coupled with frequent trips out of town for work and fun, have made it mostly okay.

With some exceptions.

I had a meltdown last year. It wasn't pretty. I'm sure, had it been filmed, I could've won some golden statuette for the performance. "And the award for *morose and irrational male attempting to communicate his needs* goes to…Scott Stabile… in *GET ME THE FUCK OUT OF PANAMA BEFORE I COMPLETELY LOSE MY SHIT!*"

I know G wished it was a fictional performance rather than a real part of his life. But there I was, twitching and screaming with the nuance and conviction of Daniel Day Lewis. A master class — in poor communication, that is.

Allow me to set the scene.

I was washing dishes when the doorbell rang. I opened the door to G, who had just returned home from a three-day work trip to Santiago, Chile. He stood there, in his pilot's uniform, captain's hat in one hand, flight bag in the other, happy to be home. I have opened the door to this picture many times, almost always excited about his return after missing him. Ordinarily, I would greet him with a hug and a kiss, grab his hat or bag, and usher him into our apartment with a "How was your flight, babe?"

This was no ordinary evening, however. Unbeknownst to G, I had already entered pre-meltdown mode. With very rare exception, pre-meltdown mode invariably leads to a full-blown meltdown. We had just passed our second anniversary of living in Panama, a year longer than we'd expected to live here, and I wanted out. *Now*. I had gotten it into my head that the city was the cause of all my problems, including my writer's block, general laziness, and overindulgence in ice cream.

So, no, I didn't much care how his flight had gone that night. I was far too busy milking my misery. He had made it home alive, and that was good enough for me (though I suspect he would have preferred the alternative more than once as the evening progressed).

"Hi, babe," he said with a smile, as yet unaware of my mood.

"I'm done. I wanna move. Seriously, I'm done. I don't like it here. You don't like it here. I can't take it anymore," I replied, choosing crazy eyes over a smile.

To that he said, "Can I come in?"

It probably goes without saying that I could have waited for him to enter our apartment, and even perhaps change out of his uniform and have a seat, before launching into my sudden need for him to quit his job and for us to sell our apartment and move to a different country. Though it's important not to put off necessary conversations just because they're difficult to have (I'm constantly putting off necessary conversations just because they're difficult to have), it's equally important to consider the timing of said conversations. I am going to be about zero percent open to listening to anyone about anything if the season finale, or any episode, really, of *Game of Thrones* is on. It's best not to dissect your sex life during the Super Bowl or bring up your desire for couples therapy as you're heading out to a holiday party. Even if nothing important is going on, mid-meltdown almost always squashes any hope of a successful communication. It does ensure unnecessary drama, though. It's hard enough for two human beings to work through their shit under the best of circumstances. And it's virtually impossible when we launch into a conversation at a bad time or with a bad attitude.

I know this, and I still chose the bad attitude.

I did step aside so G could enter our apartment. I'm not a monster. I even managed to keep my mouth shut as he took his time changing out of his uniform and stalling in our bedroom to keep from having to enter the shitstorm I'd whipped up in his absence. Who could blame him? No one walks willingly into a hurricane. Except newscasters, of course, but they wear good rain gear and get paid.

We eventually sat down on the sofa, and I did my best to communicate my frustrations peacefully and clearly. It went something like this —

"I can't believe we bought an apartment here! What were we thinking? We're total idiots! I can't stay here anymore! You stay if you want, but I'm leaving! I hate it here!"

If there's an expression that conveys "sometimes your best sucks," it applies here. I'd had three days alone to work myself into a Panama-is-evil frenzy. Make that three days plus a few months of keeping my feelings bottled up inside. Bottled-up feelings burn and rarely come out tasting good — think vomit-flavored Sriracha. The only response I was prepared to receive was one of absolute empathy and agreement. Anything short of booking our flights out of there would not suffice.

"I don't understand why it feels like such an emergency all of a sudden," G replied.

A reasonable response — to a reasonable person. I was not that person. Not right then. Reason had jumped ship and drowned while G was still up in the air, blissfully unaware of what he was coming home to. Reason was a tool of a rational mind, and I was playing in a toolshed of self-pity — frustration, disappointment, anger, sadness, and blame became my tools of choice. Basically the components of the worst communication possible.

I just wanted him to agree with me. I wanted him to feel my pain and say yes to everything I proposed. Was that too much to ask?

Of course, conversations, especially the important ones, rarely go smoothly and almost never go as planned. We come into them with our intention and expectation, hoping to get the exact outcome we're looking for. Sure, right. How often does that happen when two people are involved? I can't even talk *myself* into the outcomes I want. Good communication requires flexibility and openness. It requires a willingness to move with the flow of the conversation, without an attachment to its result. I was as flexible as steel, as open as a wall, and as detached as my head is to my body. I created no space for an actual dialogue. I wanted to make myself heard without any intention of listening to G. Less conversation and more spewing.

Not surprisingly, the more rigid I was with G, the more rigid he became with me.

"I'm not happy. Do you understand that?" I said. "We planned to stay here for a year. It's been two years. Two years in this godforsaken place!" (I am so sorry, Panama. You're beautiful, just as you are.)

"You're being seriously melodramatic," he said. *Annoying.*

"I'm not being melodramatic!" *I was totally being melodramatic.*

As he calmed himself and struggled to settle into my hysteria with some semblance of his own clarity, I resisted all his attempts at interactive dialogue.

"Let's talk through this," he suggested.

"I don't want to talk through this. We've already talked about it. I want to leave."

This wasn't the first time we'd discussed moving on from Panama. We'd had several conversations about it. Casual but real conversations. Talk of the future, of the changes we wanted to make. For me, the future had arrived, via a category 3 shitstorm, with plenty of room to intensify. I had no patience for his thoughts. I planned my responses before he even came close to finishing his. Had I spent months planning how to communicate most ineffectively, I wouldn't have done as stunning a job as I did that night. A vision, truly.

G held my hand, and I sat there in judgment of everything he had to say. In judgment of him. Like it was all his fault.

It's impossible to communicate with love and clarity when we're filled with judgment. All that comes through is frustration and anger, or worse, condemnation and disgust. It's just as hard to share our truth when we're feeling judged. We get defensive or we shut down, neither of which encourages open dialogue. I judged G, with my words and energy, which didn't create a space for him to communicate in a vulnerable and honest way. I attacked him from the moment he arrived home, and he saw defense as his only option. Attack, defend. Attack, defend. A cycle of pointlessness. All anger, no love. All war, no peace.

I couldn't switch gears. The cork had been popped. I was much too committed to my irrationality, so I continued on. As predicted, the category 3 shitstorm intensified to category 4.

"We came here for *your* job. It was just gonna be a year. You're gone half the time. You get to fly to cool cities, and I'm stuck in this place. You don't know what it's like. I'm miserable!"

Oh, yes, I did serve him up a blame casserole smothered in guilt. (If you're second guessing me as a purveyor of wisdom, well, I can hardly blame you.) I felt bad about what I was saying even as I was saying it, but I wanted to make my point, regardless. I needed to be right. That need often comes at the expense of being kind. It comes with the desire — whether consciously or not — to make others wrong in order to appease our egos. If there's anything that cripples a conversation, it's the need to be right. Still, there I was, righting the hell out of that moment, making G the villain. And there he was, working so hard to be patient and loving, and no doubt wishing he could be back in Chile, or in a Chili's, or somewhere eating chili. Anywhere but on the sofa with me.

We ended up taking a walk to dinner. Pizza. Turns out I

was starving, which definitely didn't serve the moment. Re-member timing? *Hangry* has never been my best face. Eating helped. Getting everything out of my system, even as un-gracefully as I had done it, helped. And ultimately owning my feelings and the way in which I shared them helped.

"I'm sorry. I didn't mean to attack you. I've just been feel-ing so isolated here. We don't have many friends, and I spend most of my time alone. I'm lonely. I know that's on me. I could be making more of an effort, but I don't even feel like it, maybe because it's always felt temporary. I know it's not Panama's fault that I'm unhappy, but I don't think it's helping being here."

"Let's figure it out. You know I don't need to stay here. I just don't want to rush into a decision that's gonna make our lives more difficult. I don't feel comfortable quitting my job without having something lined up."

Now, that resembled an interactive dialogue. Openness. Vulnerability. Honesty. Plenty to work with.

Though the example I've laid out in this chapter suggests otherwise, I believe one of the main reasons G and I have a strong relationship is because we often (but not always, ob-viously) communicate well with each other. Every time we're able to show up for a difficult conversation with openness, kindness, and honesty, we strengthen our relationship. We deepen our connection.

The heavy conversations are never easy, though, and we've come out of some discussions not clear if our relationship would survive. We've gone into some discussions with the same concern. Relationships are living things. They change and grow, and new conflicts present themselves, along with new reasons to grow apart or stay together. G and I are in constant conversation with each other, if not verbally then energetically. We are choosing each other, again and again, every day. The better we communicate with one another, the easier it is to make that choice.

Ultimately, we have to take responsibility for how we choose to communicate. Are we showing up with love or with judgment? Are we open to seeing where the conversation goes, or are we rigid in our expectations? Are we committed to being kind or to being right? These choices count. They invite either connection or conflict. .

Good communication empowers a relationship.

Bad communication can destroy one.

Communication, like everything else that really matters in our world, takes a shit-ton of work. We all know what it's like to walk away from conversations feeling angry, disappointed, or misunderstood. We've all regretted things we've said to people we love. We've all hurt people with our words and been hurt by the words of others. And though words matter, they never tell the whole story.

Everything is energy, and communication is no exception. Words don't always speak the truth. Think of all the times you've said something that didn't match how you felt. Have you ever replied, "Sure, that's fine," when what you really meant was "I'd rather not," or "Hell no"? Have you ever said, "Whatever you want" and meant "I can't believe you want that. I don't want that. Are you nuts?"? There are more than words at play in conversation. Energy underlies all that is spoken.

I tend to vomit everything I'm thinking when G and I sit down for an overdue conversation about something important. I'll share every nuance of my fear or frustration, just to get it all out, and that inevitably overwhelms him. He ends up thinking I'm much unhappier or more upset than I actually am. When he's not able to read my energy, which often feels much calmer than my words suggest, he ends up feeling disheartened and confused.

G tends to be a more hesitant communicator. He uses far fewer words and explains himself less pointedly. I ask him lots of questions to get him to say more, and I often feel like he's not expressing everything he needs to say. When I don't tune into his energy, I end up feeling disappointed, like he's not really sharing himself with me, even when he is.

We communicate differently. That's all. Neither is better or worse (meltdown notwithstanding); we're just different. That's why intuition is so important. And we are all intuitive, by the way. Like love and creativity, intuition is one of the great ever-present gifts of life. As is a sense of humor, when we allow it. We've got to be willing to laugh at ourselves, and at our relationships, when things get ridiculous. Well-placed humor, on its own, can relieve some of the pressure of an angry communication balloon before it bursts. G and I have laughed countless times over my hysterics that night, though, admittedly, we weren't hooting it up in the moment. That moment sucked for both of us, until we really started to communicate.

We need to listen to one another with our hearts, not just our minds. When we take in each other's words *and* really listen to each other's energy, we're able to understand one another better. Of course, we have to want to understand each other better, and be willing to accept the truth of a situation. When we get the outcome we want, it's easy to overlook what's really going on for the other person. Sometimes G tells me, "Sure, that's fine," and even though his energy tells me it's not, my desire to get my way leads me to believing his words rather than listening to his energy. (Don't judge. You know you've done the same thing!)

Sometimes he tells me he's okay when I feel he's not, and I let him know I don't think his energy matches his words, and that I'm here if he wants to talk it through. He does the same thing for me. We often need time to process things on our own — and to get honest with ourselves about how we're feeling — before we're ready to share them with someone else. Even those closest to us.

Honesty is key. When we don't bring honesty to a conversation, the entire thing becomes false. I'm not a *radical honesty* advocate, however. If we're headed to a party with no time to change, I'm not going to tell you I don't like your outfit, even if I hate your outfit. What would be the point? I'm all for white lies, when they're rooted in kindness.

Too often, however, dishonesty roots itself in fear. We don't speak our truth because we don't want to hurt the other person, or because we don't want him to judge us. We fear conflict, and we feel more comfortable interacting in falseness than in authenticity. But every time we communicate honestly, and from a place of love, we strengthen our connection with each other, no matter the outcome of the conversation. Honesty moves a relationship forward, even if forward means going our separate ways. Like everything else, honesty starts from within. Only when we can be honest with ourselves are we able to share that honesty with others. There's no saying where a connection can go when that happens.

Honestly, I don't melt down all that often, but when I do, you may as well grab some popcorn and enjoy the show. Or if the meltdown is directed at you, just excuse yourself for a moment.

Then run.

CRACKED POT

As an adult, I took piano lessons for a couple of weeks. Saxophone lessons for a month or so. One African drumming lesson. I took voice lessons for a few weeks, two different times with two different coaches. I joined a band and backed out before the first rehearsal. I stuck with method-acting classes for a couple of years. I even moved to LA to pursue acting but lost interest within a month of my arrival. I also signed up for DJ school but only went two times. I fared no better in the martial arts — two sessions of aikido, two weeks of capoeira, and two months of tae kwon do. Purple belt, thank you very much.

I've joined myriad multilevel marketing companies (sometimes called pyramid schemes), certain to get rich quick with all of them. I sold super blue-green algae, which tasted even worse than it sounds, and spent thousands of dollars on herbal products that I planned to sell but, due to inaction and expiration dates, ended up throwing away (along with my money). I became an online travel agent for a few days, and a phone service sales rep for two different phone companies in the network marketing world. I once handed $1,000 in cash over to a group of people who showed me a drawing of an actual pyramid with all our names in it. The leader of the group assured me that my $1,000 would yield me a $16,000 payoff. No products, nothing to sell. A literal pyramid scheme, and I still bought in.

I worked for a high-end gay matchmaking service for several months and became so impassioned by the prospect of finding people mates, and so disheartened by an unusually difficult boss, that I quit that job and launched my own matchmaking business called Adamo, which means "to fall in love with" in Latin. I quickly signed up my first client, a lovely sixty-something gay Episcopalian priest who wanted nothing more than to find love and paid me $12,000 to help him do so. I, however, lost my passion for matchmaking soon after taking on that first holy client and regrettably, for him, had to discontinue our business relationship, and for me, had to return his $12,000.

Not long after my stint at playing Cupid, I studied for weeks to get my California real estate license and leased a BMW I couldn't afford so that I could drive my clients around in style. I never applied for a single real estate job, though. The excitement faded the moment I passed my exam. Actually, it had faded even before the exam, but I didn't want to admit that to myself. See: BMW payments.

I've switched cities ten times and have lived in twenty-four homes in the past twenty-three years, not counting all the weeks I house-sat in my twenties to keep from having to pay rent. My Aunt Cathy called me her little gypsy, and my family members all complained about the number of times they needed to update my phone number and address in their little phone books. (Remember those?)

The point I'm making is that I lose interest easily. I can get maniacally excited about some new thing, give it my full attention for a week or two, or a day or two, and then move on from it completely. I have signed up for lessons and spent money I didn't have (thank you, credit cards) on my new passion, convinced it would be a part of my life forever. I'm a frustrating — some, though I have yet to meet them, might say delightful — blend of impulsive, delusional, and ADD-addled. My partner G always tells me he wishes we weren't a couple so he could make money selling me things I'd never use. Instead, he gets stuck spending money to buy them for me. Please don't mention the Vitamix blender to him. It was a birthday present!

If you rave to me about how the harmonica has changed your life, there's a good chance I'll go out and get a harmonica the next day, just to see if it changes mine, too. Actually, many years ago, and on the recommendation of a complete stranger I'd met in a bookstore, I tried a self-taught harmonica tutorial. For an hour. (It didn't change my life.)

I'd never liked this aspect of my personality. Because I never stuck with anything, I felt like I was failing all the time, like I had no follow-through, and I judged that as bad. As lazy, immature, and unreliable. (Wait, are you nodding in agreement?) Even so, like a dog chasing a squirrel, I ran after the next life-changing experience the moment it presented itself.

And inevitably lost interest. This "flaw" in my character, as I saw it, contributed to intense feelings of disappointment and shame.

What's wrong with me? I wondered. *How can I fix this part of myself?*

I had accepted that my impulsive, delusional, ADD ways meant that I was broken.

● ● ●

One of my favorite parables — which I've seen credited as an Indian and a Chinese folktale — tells the story of a cracked pot. I don't know where it originated, and I haven't been to India or mainland China, so I'm going to set it in the mountains of Bali, one of my favorite places on the planet.

As my version of the story goes, a bold Balinese woman named Nyoman lived alone in a wooden cabin high up in the mountains near Ubud. Each morning, she trudged more than two miles to the closest stream to gather water for drinking, cooking, and bathing. She carried with her two large clay pots, which she had crafted specifically for the purpose of carrying water. She'd painted one pot purple and the other pink, but only because she'd run out of her favorite black and silver paints.

Every morning, she hung the pots on a long bamboo pole, one pot at each end of the pole, then rested the pole across her neck and shoulders in order to carry the clay pots back and forth between her cabin and the stream. The journey mostly sucked, especially the return. Who wants to lug two giant pots

full of water more than two miles up a mountainside? Not
Nyoman, but she needed the water.

At least she adored her pots. They loved her, too.

"Thank you, dear pots, for the gift of water each day," she
said, each time she returned home from the stream before col-
lapsing onto her bed, sweaty and exhausted.

"It is a great honor to serve you, dear Nyoman," the pots
replied, because in parables such as this, clay pots don't just
talk but do so with refined formality.

One day, upon returning home with her pots, Nyoman
was surprised to see the purple pot only half full of water.
"What the f—" Before she had a chance to finish her thought,
which may or may not have been profane, she noticed a crack
on the side of the pot, where the water must have escaped.
"Hmm," she thought. "Interesting."

The purple pot sensed its crack and knew it had arrived
home only half full. Though it felt disappointed by this, it
didn't panic, hopeful it would retain all its water the next time.

The following day, however, the purple pot returned half
full once again. The day after that, too. Then the performance
anxiety really set in. In fact, for more than a year, Nyoman
filled the pots, as she always did at the stream's edge, and the
purple pot returned with only half its water, causing it great
distress. To make matters worse, the pink pot, which always
returned home full, had grown a little, well, full of itself. When
Nyoman went to sleep, the pink pot teased the purple pot.
"Pull up your pants," the pink pot whispered. "I can see your
crack." The pink pot laughed, but the purple pot sulked even
more.

One morning, as warm sunshine blessed the mountain, Nyoman returned home with her pots and thanked them, as usual. "Thank you, dear pots, for the gift of water each day."

"It is a great honor to serve you, dear Nyoman," the pink pot replied.

The purple pot, however, burst into tears. "I'm so sorry, dear Nyoman. I've failed you over and over again. I am a worthless pot!"

"Failed me? Worthless?" Nyoman didn't understand. "Did you take acting classes when I wasn't looking, because you sure have gotten dramatic!" Nyoman laughed wildly at her tired joke while massaging her tired feet.

The purple pot just frowned, because obviously pots that talk and cry can also frown.

"I am cracked and no longer worthy of your care. For more than a year I have not been able to provide you with a full load of water. Every morning, the moment we leave the stream I feel the water begin to seep out through the crack in my side, and I know I will disappoint you again. Please craft yourself a new pot, one that will not fail you so."

Nyoman held the pot in her hands and smiled. "My dear purple pot, you need to chill, for real. You haven't disappointed me at all."

"But I am no good," the pot insisted. "I am a cracked pot."

"You and me both, honey," Nyoman replied. "I need to show you something." She carried the purple pot outside and walked with it along the path to the stream. "Do you see all the wildflowers along your side of the path?" she asked. "All these Balinese beauties?"

The purple pot took in the yellow- and rose-tinted plumeria, the violet bluebells, and the fiery red ixora flowers that colored its side of the path. It even spotted some wild jasmine shrubs, their simple white flowers salted among all the color. The pot's journey to and from the stream had been clouded with so much guilt and shame that it had never noticed the flowers until this moment. "I see them," the pot replied.

"Do you see any flowers on the other side of the path?" Nyoman asked. "The side under which the pink pot travels each day?"

The purple pot looked to the pink pot's side of the path but saw no flowers, just bare mountainside. "I don't understand," the pot said. "Why are there flowers only on my side of the path?"

Nyoman chuckled. "Because, drama queen, the morning after I noticed your crack, I planted seeds along your side of the path. Every day, as we return home from the stream, you water them. What used to be empty ground now bursts with color because of you. At least now, when I make the back-breaking journey to and from the stream each day, I get to take in the beauty and scent of all these flowers! All because of your crack. Got it?"

The purple pot listened to Nyoman in disbelief. It stared out at the blanket of flowers it had played a part in creating, and it wept, like no pot — purple or pink or black or silver — had ever wept before. It had only ever seen its crack as a flaw but now understood that it was also a gift.

"Thank you, dear Nyoman," it said. "It is my great honor to serve you."

● ● ●

Though it still frustrates me at times, I've grown to appreciate — even love — the part of my personality that jumps from one thing to the next. Better to have played an African drum once than never to have played an African drum at all. I'm more gifted at trying new things than I am at sticking with them. That's just who I am. It's one of the cracks that makes me, me. I've met many interesting people this way and have played in all sorts of different worlds. My crack has grown endless flowers and friendships, including the priest, my piano teacher, my acting coach, and even the guy who brought me into that $16,000 pyramid scheme.

I was talking about this chapter with my friend Susan, and she reminded me that had I not dragged her to a Teach for America informational session in college, she may never have worked with that organization and become a teacher. I, of course, was dead set on becoming a Teach for America teacher, too, but lost interest before finishing the application (it was really long).

Susan went on to teach elementary school for twenty years. Sometimes our cracks lead others to their flowers, too.

Which of your cracks have you spent too much time judging?

How might your "flaws" actually be adding to the beauty of our world?

We can waste our lives feeling guilty and ashamed over aspects of our appearance or personality that we can't control or that we can control but feel less free when we do so.

Whatever we consciously repress only oppresses us in return. We can hide ourselves because of our perceived flaws. Or we can embrace the flaws. We can choose to see the ways in which our cracks add beauty to the world around us and the ways in which they enhance our own lives. We can choose to recognize that whatever makes us who we are is something to celebrate, not suppress. Without needing them to define us, we can begin to let our cracks give us a bit more definition.

Then, like the flowers we're bound to inspire, we can finally, fully bloom.

ROOMIE

I found out from his Facebook page that my friend Kevin had died. I'd emailed him twice with a question I needed answered and hadn't heard back from him. At first I assumed he was traveling (he was always on a plane to somewhere) but knew something was wrong when a week passed after the second email with no response. That was completely unlike him. He worked on his computer every day and was usually quick to respond to messages. Fearing the worst, I thought to check his Facebook page.

I took a deep, nervous breath and clicked on his profile.

Please don't let him be dead. Please don't let him be dead.

This was the first post I saw on his page: "With Kevin leaving us I am reminded of how fragile life is. I saw some movie, I don't remember what it was, but there was this line at the end of it: *What is the greatest thing we can do for one another? Be aware of one another. Be conscious of one another. Do not walk blindly through the day as you pass your brothers and sisters on the street.* Godspeed, Kevin. Wherever this has taken you,

I pray it is a place of joy and light and that you feel free and happy."

Kevin was dead. Just like that. My dread of finding out that he had died didn't prevent the shock. Through tears, I read all the comments left by all Kevin's other friends, everyone stunned and saddened that he was no longer with us. Many shared happy memories of Kevin, and all had glowing things to say about their friend. I learned more about Kevin's adventurous and philanthropic past and felt even deeper love and respect for him through their comments.

I wondered how many of them had learned of his death on that page, as I had. If not for Facebook, how many of us would still have imagined Kevin to be out there doing whatever it was we each knew him to do? I wondered how many of his friends still had no idea he had died.

I searched within the comments for an explanation of his death but found none. Though it wouldn't have changed anything, I needed to know how he'd died — as though his death couldn't be entirely real without my knowing the cause. Is it possible to learn that someone died without asking, "How?" or "What happened?" Is it possible to accept death as is, with no further explanation? It wasn't for me.

My fear roared stronger than my curiosity: I hoped it wasn't a prescription drug overdose.

I knew it was a prescription drug overdose.

I messaged the man who posted the movie quote to find out what had happened to my friend. He responded immediately, letting me know that Kevin had in fact overdosed on prescription drugs a month earlier. His realtor found him dead on his bedroom floor. No one knew for sure whether Kevin had killed himself intentionally or by accident, though authorities suspected suicide. Not that it mattered, really. Both possibilities felt equally tragic, either that he could've been so desperate and lonely he wanted to take his own life or that he could've been so lost in his addiction he killed himself against his will. I wanted to believe it was an accident, though. I wanted to believe he never stopped loving himself, and that he never gave up hope. And though it was difficult for me to imagine that Kevin could have considered suicide, I knew better than to rule it out. It's impossible to know what's really going on in someone else's mind, even those closest to us, even when they share their struggles.

I replayed the words of the first post I read: *Be aware of one another.... Do not walk blindly through the day as you pass your brothers and sisters on the street.* The words stung. I'd been acutely aware of Kevin's addiction to prescription drugs and chose, for a long time, to ignore it. To walk blindly around it. Now my friend was dead, and I'd found out on his fucking Facebook page, an entire month after he'd ODed.

● ● ●

I moved in with Kevin in January 2007 and spent two years in his hillside Marin County home, barely twenty minutes north of San Francisco. The first time I visited his house, he and I got along so well we ended up going to lunch after I looked at the room for rent.

"I think we'll be good roommates," he told me, over salads.

"I don't need to check any references. The room's yours if you want it."

I wanted it.

I rented a furnished bedroom in his basement, with a lovely view of the city across the bay. I had my own bathroom and office space, and a charming downstairs living room all to myself. Kevin and I became friends. We shared meals on occasion, gave each other dating advice, and watched more than a few BBC wildlife specials together. "I could watch penguins do absolutely nothing for days," he declared. I agreed.

We weren't especially close friends but we cared about each other. I drove him to the emergency room during an anxiety attack that had him convinced he was having a stroke. He cut the price of my rent for a few months when my money was tight. We looked out for each other. He worked at home as a corporate event producer, the kitchen table his office. I worked as the development guy for a local production company, pitching show ideas to networks like National Geographic and Discovery Channel. He spent most of his time at home, and I spent very little time there. In many ways, we shared a perfect living situation — a lot of respect and a lot of space.

Kevin struggled with insomnia, anxiety, and chronic lower back pain from a slipped disc. He took prescription meds for each of these conditions. He'd put his trust in a psychiatrist to come up with a drug cocktail that would alleviate his ailments. And it worked. He eventually became too doped up to feel much of anything. As months passed, I'd often come home to a somewhat disoriented, slurring version of my roommate —

a stark contrast to the insightful, intelligent, and eloquent man I'd come to know.

Kevin and I had a couple of conversations about his meds. "Maybe you should look for a different psychiatrist," I gently encouraged, "at least to get a second opinion about all your prescriptions." I told him I worried about his health, and though I believed he was addicted, I never suggested it. I put the responsibility on the doctor rather than on him, fearing he would become defensive and shut down if I hinted at addiction. I didn't want to invite conflict. It's amazing how much harder it is to be a good friend when being a good friend calls for more than commiseration, laughter, or BBC wildlife specials. But isn't that one of the truest signs of friendship — being willing to piss off your friend, and even jeopardize your connection, because you care more about his well-being than anything else?

Kevin told me he planned to wean himself off the meds eventually but that his anxiety and back pain especially were too debilitating to do things differently yet. "I'm not ready," he said. I mostly believed him. I'd seen the effects of his anxiety in more than one panic attack, and I'd watched him limp around the house at times and shriek in pain from his back. He wasn't faking either condition. Still, I listened to my mind judge him for all the medication he took and frequently complained to my partner about Kevin's habits.

It's easy to judge people for their choices when we haven't walked in their shoes. Who was I to condemn Kevin for wanting to be comfortable? I couldn't relate to that degree of panic or pain but suspected that I, too, would want something to alleviate both if that were me. Nobody likes to suffer.

I knew Kevin was addicted to his painkillers and that he was in denial, but I never mentioned it to him while I was living there. Even though he often slurred his speech. Even though he'd binge-eat in the middle of the night with no recollection of having woken up. Even though it had gotten increasingly difficult to catch him in an entirely lucid state. I didn't want to get involved. I didn't want to invest myself in his story. I didn't want my world to be consumed by substance abuse. Not again. I grew up in a world of addiction and wanted nothing to do with Kevin's. It was easier for me to hide out in the basement and pretend that all was well, that he would get himself together eventually.

I knew I wasn't to blame for Kevin's death any more than I was to blame for his addiction. We can never own the choices of another. I felt guilty, though. I could have been a much better friend. I could have cared more about his well-being than I did about my comfort. I could have put his health first, even if suggesting addiction meant being asked to leave his home, or being asked to support him through his recovery, or being asked to accept his habits as they were. It's not for us to decide how others take care of themselves.

I could have done something more than nothing.

I eventually did.

● ● ◐

About two years before his death, while I was living in Brooklyn with my partner, Kevin and I had a long conversation over the phone. He talked about a fight he'd had with a cousin over his prescription drug usage. He'd awakened in the middle of the night and had ravaged several desserts his cousin had prepared for the next day's Thanksgiving dinner. "I ate the entire pumpkin pie," he laughed. "And half the cheesecake."

His cousin exploded and told him she wanted no contact with him until he cleaned himself up — from drugs and alcohol, which he admitted he'd been consuming more and more of in recent months.

"She's always been uptight," he said, "and I was sick of it, anyway." He took no responsibility for his actions, and neither of us made any references to his drug use. I didn't speak up in the moment but knew I wouldn't stay silent any longer, especially because Kevin seemed increasingly lost and unhappy.

Once we hung up, I wrote him an email. I told Kevin I thought he had a serious drug problem and that he was in denial, that he needed to find a new psychiatrist, and that his life was not going to improve until he made some drastic changes regarding his prescription drug habit. I told him I loved him and was there if he needed me, even though a large part of me hoped he wouldn't need me, that he'd handle it on his own or with the support of other friends. I kept seeing flashes of my brother and father, remembering all the trauma their addictions caused our family.

I went back and forth over whether to send the email. It's hard to speak the truth when the truth is going to hurt or when you're not sure it's going to make any difference. And what if Kevin did need me, even more than I'd imagined? What if he needed me as an anchor in his sobriety? I worried

I might be committing myself to his life in a way that didn't feel comfortable.

I sent the email.

Kevin responded by email a week later. To my surprise, he agreed with everything I'd written and thanked me for writing it. Since receiving my email, he'd already reached out to a new psychiatrist, as well as a psychotherapist. He had begun to make changes and said that he planned to work hard to get himself off the meds. I felt relieved by his openness and happy to know he was taking action to heal himself. Though I'd waited such a long time to bring up his addiction, and only said something once I was living across the country, safe from having to play too present a role in his journey, I still felt grateful to eventually have found the courage, and the love, to send the email. It seemed to have helped him in some way.

● ● ●

I don't judge alcohol and drug addiction anymore, but I still notice myself shutting down around it, particularly when an addicted person has no interest in getting sober. Not that he has to want to get sober. We make it through this life however we can. That choice is his alone. Still, I want to sprint in the other direction, away from all the painful triggers addiction calls up in me — away from the choices of my heroin-addicted brother and my gambling-addicted father. I lived my childhood, in great part, in a world of addiction, on the receiving end of the unstable actions of addicts. Though addiction became the norm in our home, I was always aware, even as a child, of the damage my father and brother caused because of their choices.

I see how my past influenced my choices with Kevin. So often we find ourselves unwilling to face a present reality because we know, consciously or subconsciously, we'll also have to face the past. The hardest experiences of our lives never stop living with us. They move forward into our day-to-day existence, and we are left to decide how we want to integrate the pain. Do we build walls to hide it or open doors to face it? Walls have helped me survive when I've needed them, but they've played no part in my healing. Still, I built a wall around Kevin's addiction for a long time so I wouldn't have to look through the open door of my childhood, to heroin and gambling and lies and death.

I know that's okay, and that we show up however we're able to show up for whatever situation presents itself. Healthy boundaries matter, too, especially in our friendships. We can't always give what needs to be given. Still, I wish I had shown up stronger with Kevin sooner, even though I know it may not have made any difference at all. He would always have been the only person deciding his fate.

● ● ●

As far as I knew, after his response to my email, Kevin had been doing really well. I had lunch with him in New York about six months before his death, and he looked great. He had put on some weight since I'd last seen him, with a belly that seemed to me reflective of someone choosing food over drugs. He was energetic, optimistic, and refreshingly lucid. The months passed with a couple of quick texts back and forth but not much real interaction. And then he was dead, alone on his bedroom floor for who knows how long before his realtor discovered his body. I've tried to consider how lonely and afraid he must have felt in those moments, days, and months before he died. I still want to believe it was an accident.

It was Kevin's birthday recently. I know, because Facebook reminded me, its algorithm obviously unaware of Kevin's death. I clicked on his page to spend a little time with my friend. Scattered among a handful of *missing you* posts were dozens of *Happy Birthday, Kevin!* posts by those who clearly still had no idea he'd died — they still imagined him at his kitchen table surrounded by stacks of paper, or on his yearly flight to Australia, or planning some corporate or philanthropic event. To these friends, Kevin lived on. Lucky them.

I scrolled until I found the post from two years before that told me of Kevin's death, and I reread the words that had so struck me: *Be aware of one another. Be conscious of one another. Do not walk blindly through the day as you pass your brothers and sisters on the street.*

I'd like to believe I'd act differently today if put in the same situation, but I don't honestly know. We think we've learned lessons, until we're given another chance, until we're made to act. Then we see what we have or haven't learned. I would hope to be more up front with my feelings and less inclined to put up a wall, even if I felt the need to create certain boundaries within the experience. Walls and boundaries are not the same thing; walls shut people out entirely, while boundaries invite them in, with conditions.

I'm working hard at being more real with my friends, and more available — at saying the tough things, at holding up a mirror, and at staying open to their truth when they share it with me. I fail at friendship constantly, however. I catch myself all the time biting my tongue, becoming defensive, retreating — because I worry about how my words will land, or because I'm not in the mood for a difficult conversation, or because I fear my friends won't like me as much afterward.

I want to be a better friend than that. A more fearless friend. A less selfish friend. A friend driven by love, no matter what, and by the desire to see those I love living their best possible lives, whatever that means for them. When I had that final lunch with Kevin in New York, I felt excited to see him back on track, optimistic that he had rediscovered the path to some version of his best possible life.

Kevin was a good man — kind and smart and so very quirky. I feel lucky to have spent a couple of years as his roommate, lucky to have shared space with a man who cared for others, even when he could no longer manage to care for himself. I miss him.

I won't stop working at being a better friend. I'll keep pushing myself to act from love, even when love demands the most difficult conversations, or interrupts my routine, or calls on me to give more than I thought I could give. That's the thing about love: it's clear. When we put our trust in its instructions and follow its lead closely, we don't need to think as much about what we're doing or worry that we're doing it all wrong. We just have to be present in its energy and listen to however it's asking us to show up.

Then, we have to show up.

SCAREDY-CAT

spent an entire day in LA with Elizabeth Gilbert and Rob Bell, two writers / thinkers / love warriors / humans warming our world with their generous hearts. Kind, wise, funny, and real, they both hover near the top of my *favorite people list*. I'd love to say the three of us brunched together at an organic eatery in Venice Beach and then hiked sunny Runyon Canyon all afternoon, where we regaled each other with creativity tips, spiritual parables, and R-rated jokes. *There once was a monk from Nantucket....* The truth is, I was just one of about four hundred other lucky souls gathered with them — at their daylong event in Hollywood. It was more hangout than workshop. The two friends sat onstage, on stools, and told stories and answered questions, sharing their wisdom and love with a roomful of superfans. I even landed in the front row, because the two equally geeked-out friends I met there arrived early and snatched us some prime seats. Don't be jealous, but I could practically touch Elizabeth Gilbert's stool. (That sounds absolutely disgusting out of context.)

Along with all their storytelling and question answering, Elizabob (their celebrity friendship name) gave us six assignments that day: to write six different letters. The first letter — which happens to launch this chapter perfectly — they told us to write to ourselves, from our fear. Elizabob encouraged us to stay as open as possible to whatever our fear wanted us to know.

Turns out, my fear had a lot on its mind. Its letter went something like this.

Dear Scott,

I am your Fear, and this is what I need to tell you.

This world is not a friendly place, and I don't want you to get hurt. That's why I want you to be quiet and less opinionated. That's why I keep trying to stop you from sharing yourself. I'm afraid others won't like or be able to make sense out of what you're saying and doing. I worry people will judge you, and then you'll only judge yourself harder. My job is to protect you, to keep you safe and comfortable. I fear people will call you names, and I don't want you to be condemned by others. The homophobes are bad enough, aren't they?

I'm afraid the more open you allow yourself to be, the more sensitive you'll continue to become, and then life will just become more and more uncomfortable for you. I worry you can't handle all the pain in this world, which is why I push you to escape rather than bear witness and feel. I don't want you to be crushed under the weight of this planet's violence and rage. I would rather you be blind to it, for your own good. I just don't want you to feel as anxious as you do.

I'm scared that people are going to judge your creativity and call you a hack, or judge your spirituality and call you a fraud. I worry people are going to say you're full of shit and make fun of you, and then you'll feel like even more of an outsider than you've already felt for most of your life. Always an orphan.

I'm afraid you'll never create something you truly love. I push you to stop creating just so you won't be disappointed by the outcome. I'm scared you'll never be...

Time ran out. My fear, no doubt, could have gone on for hours.

Maybe your fear speaks a similar language?

Maybe you could relate to some of what my fear had to tell me?

I loved writing that letter and have since integrated the exercise into some of my own workshops. (Thanks, Elizabob!) I've allowed my fear to write me several letters since that day, sometimes surprised by, and always appreciative of, what it needed to say. I'd given my fear so much power all my life without ever having really given it a clear voice, without ever having listened to the concern behind its demands. I encourage you to write yourself a letter from your fear (right now — or soon — would be great), and to stay as open and accepting as you can to everything your fear wants to tell you. Let it explain why it acts the way it does.

If you're anything like me, you haven't gotten along too well with your fear up to now. You two may spend a lot of time together, but I doubt you're very friendly. It doesn't have to be that way. We can create a different, gentler relationship with our fear, and by doing so we create a more fulfilling relationship with ourselves.

I've hated my fear for all the limitations it's placed on my life. I've resented it for influencing my choices and pushing me to make cowardly decisions that have steered me away from rather than toward exciting possibilities and more meaningful realities. I've judged my fear a bully, a tyrant, the single greatest obstacle to my happiness. I had never considered that my fear cared about me or that it had always been, in fact, just trying to protect me, the only way it knew how. Don't get me wrong. I still consider my fear a serious pain in the ass, but it no longer scares me the way it used to.

My fear is just a dummy most of the time. So is yours. It doesn't mean to be, but it doesn't know any better. Fear takes its job — to protect us — incredibly seriously, but it has no emotional intelligence with which to work. My fear wants to protect me from a difficult conversation with the same fervor it uses to keep me from sprinting into traffic. Fear can't tell if it's a mountain lion or a cute barista that has you all worked up. It deems anything uncomfortable as unsafe and, therefore, something to avoid. Rattlesnakes, job changes, new hairstyles — they're all the same to fear: scary. So our fear ignites terror in our minds — a hellfire of *what-ifs* — to keep us safely in our comfort zones. More accurately, in its comfort zone. It's not so much an enemy as an overprotective parent. And like any overprotective parent, fear has no intention of giving us our space.

I finally accepted that my fear had no plans to go away. That I would not, someday, suddenly become fearless. So many times, I'd stopped myself from taking action because I felt afraid — of rejection, of change, of failure, of the unknown. I didn't ask the charming guy for his number, or didn't get out of the unhealthy relationship soon enough, or didn't submit my short story to the competition, or didn't quit my miserable job. I let my fear prevent me from making positive choices, often telling myself I would make them when I felt less afraid — when I had become fearless about the decision. But I never became fearless; I rarely even became less afraid. So I stayed paralyzed in situations that didn't serve my happiness, or I bypassed opportunities that likely would have benefited my life.

Can you relate? Have you ever held out on making a necessary change until you felt less scared to make it and ended up not making the change at all? Change will always be scary. Fearlessness will always be a myth. We can be afraid and still make courageous choices. Courage doesn't even exist without an element of fear. *It's action with fear that makes a choice brave.*

I've long been a pro at being scared, and I'm finally becoming expert at making brave choices, despite the fear. When we recognize that our fear only wants to protect us, that it's a total dummy, and that it's not going anywhere, we can begin to have different conversations with it. We can relate more openly to its needs, without sacrificing our own. I view my fear as an annoying five-year-old, tugging on my shirt and whining mostly nonsensical concerns at me all day. Instead of swearing at it, cowering in front of it, or warring with it, as I have all my life, I've taken to shooing my fear away. "Okay, okay, I heard you. Now go play in the corner or something."

Then I get on with being courageous. Because this is my one life, and I'll be damned if I'll allow my fear to keep me from realizing my best life possible. Been there, done that. Not anymore, thank you. That ship has not only sailed, it's been struck by lightning, engulfed in a hurricane, and swallowed by the sea. *Bon voyage.*

I loved what Rob Bell had to say about fear at the event in LA. When his fear plays out all the reasons he shouldn't do what he's thinking of doing and all the potential disasters, he simply nods his head and, with wonder and possibility, responds to his fear, "I know!" What a great response, right? He doesn't ignore his fear, because that's not possible. He acknowledges it with openness and acceptance of the many potential nightmares it proposes. Then he responds. His "I know!" is my "Okay, okay, I heard you. Now go play in the corner or something." Both answers attempt to make one thing clear: "Yes, I'm afraid, and no, I will not allow my fear to keep me from taking this creative/important/brave/necessary action I need to take." Find whatever response to your fear works best for you, as long as it keeps you moving forward, making the courageous choices you know you need to make for yourself and for your life.

Action helps assuage fear. The moment I signed the contract for this book, I spun out in terror. "You won't be able to finish the book in time," my fear told me. "The pressure is going to get you, and you'll have nothing good to say. Your editor's going to be disappointed, and the critics will savage you. It's not too late to back out, Scott." My fear had shape-shifted from an annoying five-year-old into an apocalyptic warlord. I panicked, and then panicked some more, and then started writing the book. Every day, I showed up at my computer — with my fear *and* with my commitment to write. And every day, I wrote. My fear never left, but it got the message, that I intended to write the book no matter what it said. It eventually quieted down. It's hard to tell someone he can't do something while he's in the midst of doing it. I've been too busy writing the book to focus on my fear of not being able to write the book. Take action, and fear usually falls in line.

I've often felt too afraid and paralyzed to take action, because the prospect of what I wanted to create or achieve seemed impossibly huge. When I signed the book contract, I couldn't imagine actually finishing the book (don't tell my editor). I stood at A, and my goal of a completed book — let's call it Z — cast its oppressive shadow over the entire path. How would I be able to do everything I needed to do in order to write the book, in order to reach Z? But the thing is, I didn't need to do everything; I only needed to do one thing at a time. The first step from A only needs to land us at B, not at Z. From B, we only need to find our way to C. Then C leads us to D. Suddenly, we're standing at R, and Z has started to look

mighty attainable. I didn't sit down to write all of *Big Love*
each day. I sat down to work on whatever chapter I'd planned
to work on. Letter by letter, word by word, paragraph by paragraph. Eventually, I finished the book (at least, I'm assuming I
did, because obviously I'm still writing it).

If you're feeling completely freaked out by the prospect
of making a big change and by all the steps necessary to make
that change happen, deconstruct the situation. Make it more
palatable to your fear. The next step to fulfilling a dream may
actually be just sending an email or making a phone call. You
can do that. Even your fear may not bitch too much about an
email. Then take whatever step you need to take after that.
One at a time. You'll gradually find your way to your goal.

While you're at it, consider your comfort throughout.
Don't just reject possibilities by saying, "I'm too scared to do
this." Instead, ask yourself the following question: "Knowing
that I'm going to be scared, what can I do to make this situation as comfortable as possible?" Whenever I speak in front
of a crowd, I know I'm going to be cold-sweating in terror
on the day of the talk, until the moment I start to speak (and
sometimes until I'm done). One of my biggest fears when I
speak is running out of things to say. So I arrive with much
more material than I would ever need, which helps me calm
that fear (and foolishly agree to more speaking gigs). Look at
what aspects frighten you, and consider everything you can
do to make them less scary. By taking care of ourselves in this
way, we set ourselves up to make more brave choices. We get
ourselves that much closer to Z, that much more comfortably.

I would love to be able to tell you that the more you face

your fear, the less fear you'll have to face. You may be lucky in that regard, but that hasn't been the case for me. I'm still a big scaredy-cat. I push myself beyond my comfort zone all the time these days, and it continues to be frightening and uncomfortable. I've done hundreds of live videos on my Facebook page, and I get nervous every single time — even when I'm just signing on to say hello. I find that fact exciting, though. In the past, I would have let those nerves, that palpable fear, stop me from doing the videos. I would have relented to my fear. Not anymore. My fear has so much less control over the choices I make than it's ever had before, simply because I don't give it the power I used to. I hear its concerns, and I shoo it away. I remind myself that it's just trying to protect me but that it's not very bright or insightful. Then, because I may be afraid but I am also brave, determined, and oh so resilient, I get busy kicking ass at my life. Ever the fearful warrior.

THE HAPPINESS
CHALLENGE

I'm a big fan of happiness.

Shocking, I know. That's like proclaiming, "I'm a big fan of peace, or love, or chocolate." Obvious much? We all want to be happy, as often as possible.

Although happiness is a common objective, it's never a given. Being alive doesn't automatically equal being happy. It often equals the opposite. Regular tastes of happiness take intentional choice and concentrated effort. Even then, unfortunately, it's not a sure thing. Effort definitely improves our odds of finding happiness, however, and it beats sitting on our butts waiting to be struck by joy.

We have to be willing to work for the things we want, right?

With that in mind, I announced a Happiness Challenge on my Facebook page. I asked the community to consider the following question: *What is one thing you will do every day in February that serves your happiness and well-being? What one thing will you do, every day, that speaks to your willingness to take care of yourself?*

I chose February, because it's the shortest month of the year and thus automatically improved our odds of finishing the challenge. Self-care is damned hard work. I'm for any shortcuts that help make it easier.

I committed to doing at least one hour of yoga each day for the month. Though I love how yoga makes me feel, I'd never stuck with a consistent practice. Like doing Pilates, eating spirulina, or swishing coconut oil in my mouth for twenty minutes each morning (oil pulling, anyone?), yoga became one more holistic practice to skip. I wanted to change that trend.

Many members of my Facebook community took the challenge — one planned to take photos of each sunrise throughout the month, another committed to painting daily, and another to dancing around her apartment for at least ten minutes every day. Several joined me in a yoga commitment. Several more vowed to walk or jog each day. A whole bunch chose meditation as their challenge. One woman, who struggled to relax, committed to doing absolutely nothing for at least twenty minutes every single day. She planned to sit on her butt, close her eyes or stare at the wall, and do nothing. That is *so* not a challenge for me, by the way, and is, in fact, how I spend some part of most days. I'm quite expert at doing not a thing.

February arrived, and the challenge began. I checked in daily with words of encouragement and to report my own progress. I was downward-dogging like a champ. Many community members shared their progress as well. We kept each other energized, and it made a difference. It's usually more fun, and motivating, to take on a challenge with others. I'm about a thousand times more inclined to show up at the gym if I'm meeting a workout partner there. Five thousand times more inclined if we're meeting at a bakery, but whatever. With the Happiness Challenge, I felt accountable to the community, and it kept me focused.

I did yoga every day that month and kept up my practice three to four times a week after that, for a few more months. Um, anyway, let's just say I'm off the yoga kick for now. (But I did start swishing coconut oil again last week!) The challenge, however, confirmed some things about happiness for me.

Happiness is not a choice. Really, it's not.

If it were, who would ever choose to be angry or jealous or depressed?

Wouldn't we all be choosing happiness all the time?

I used to believe that happiness was a choice. In my book, *Just Love*, I even wrote the following: *Happiness is work. So is misery. Both are choices. Only one comes with smiles.* It's not that simple, though.

I believed that if we focused hard enough on being happy, we would, in fact, become happy. That all moments offered the possibility of choosing happiness. Of course, I couldn't understand why I found myself unhappy so much of the time. Shouting to the heavens, "I choose happiness!" didn't seem to be making any difference to all my other emotions.

My Anger just scoffed, "You can scream all you want about happiness, but you're mine today, and *pissed off* is on the menu."

"I'm gonna need some time with him after you," my Sadness mumbled.

"Not before we complain about the state of this effed-up world," grumbled my Disgust.

If human beings weren't designed to feel all the emotions, all those emotions wouldn't exist. And that's the thing: happiness is an emotion. A feeling. We can be choosy about our thoughts, but we can't choose our feelings. We feel how we feel, no matter what we think. Just consider all the times you've tried to think yourself out of feeling something. It doesn't work. If a loved one dies, or your partner leaves you, you're not going to be able to think yourself away from feeling sad about it. If you get fired from your job for no good reason, you can't think yourself out of anger or fear. Thoughts and emotions are different animals. If our thoughts are domesticated horses that we can often manipulate, our emotions are wild stallions, free and unpredictable.

The idea that we can choose happiness has taken the personal-development world by storm. The problem there, for everyone not lucky enough to be happy all the time — which is all of us — is that we begin to think we're doing something wrong when we're not glowing with joy. We convince ourselves we are flawed somehow, or that we've missed the happiness ship in this lifetime. So we become disappointed and sad. I'd often attached happiness to my spiritual growth. I believed my inability to live in constant unbridled joy suggested I wasn't nearly as spiritually evolved as I thought myself to be. Full disclosure: I realize several times a day I'm not as spiritually evolved as I think myself to be, but that has nothing to do with my happiness level.

Many of us put unnecessary pressure on ourselves to be happy all the time. I used to be the consummate Pollyanna, always smiling, relentlessly optimistic, full of "It's all good, bro." That's some serious bro-shit. It's not always all good, and it doesn't need to be. That's not how life works, not if you're a human being with a human heart and mind.

Optimism is great, but not at the expense of authenticity. I'll take real over happy, most days, anyway. I walked around for much of my life with a perma-smile plastered on my face — in part because I have a naturally positive attitude, for which I'm grateful. And in part because I wasn't willing to look at the fullness of my life honestly enough to account for my shadow. My smile spent much of its time on the surface, refusing to acknowledge my pain. I don't believe there's a Pollyanna alive without a landfill of pain beneath all that joy. Sometimes we use happiness as a defense against the world. We smile to keep from having to feel. That's okay, but it's still a wall, one that prevents us from realizing an even deeper, truer happiness.

Don't worry, all is not lost in the world of happiness and choice.

I launched the Happiness Challenge not to suggest that we can choose happiness but to remind us that we can make choices that stand a good chance of leading to happiness. The more we do things that tend to make us happy, the happier we're likely to become. That's common sense, right? *One-plus-one-equals-two* spirituality.

I love to play tennis. It usually makes me happy (unless I'm playing like total crap). Generally, I know that by choosing to play tennis, I'm likely to evoke happiness. I'm not choosing happiness, I'm choosing to play tennis. There's a difference. We may not be able to choose our emotions, but we can choose the actions we take that affect our emotions. When I decide to watch a YouTube video I love, I invite happiness. When I decide to read the comments below that video, I invite anger. When I'm more selective about the invitations I put out into the world — and focus on those things that bring me joy — I invite a more peaceful, contented life.

Do you want to experience more happiness?

If yes, what are you doing to make that happen?

(If no, maybe skip to the next chapter.)

Are you choosing habits, activities, and relationships that support your desire for more happiness? If not, no problem, you can start right now. What tends to make you smile and feel good? If it's fresh air, then get outside every day, even for five minutes. If it's bowling, then drag a friend to the lanes once a week, or join a league. If it's good conversation, then pick up the phone and call someone you love, someone who makes you laugh. If it's reading, then read a ... wait, you're doing that!

We don't have to imagine making positive choices. Instead, we can just make them. I can't count the number of times I've said to myself, "I need to get outside more." Well, outside is literally just on the other side of my door. That desire is absolutely within my power. Consider all the positive choices that are within your power right now. Even spending five minutes a day focused on activities that bring us joy

THE HAPPINESS CHALLENGE 131

makes a difference. It's five more minutes spent feeding your soul. It's also an energetic declaration that you matter enough to yourself to invite the possibility of happiness into your life.

The desire for more happiness also requires us to pay attention to the habits, activities, and relationships that *don't* support our well-being. What choices are we making that direct us away from the possibility of happiness? When we become aware of these choices, and clear about how they make us feel, we empower ourselves to stop making them. Awareness always comes first. Whenever I eat a pint of ice cream in one sitting, I end up feeling like crap. Can you imagine that? Knowing this, it's up to me to put down the pint before I've inhaled it all. If I choose not to, I'm also choosing to steer myself away from the possibility of happiness (and to the probability of diarrhea — sorry, that's gross but true).

What choices are you making that don't serve the possibility of happiness? What habits can you consider altering or getting rid of completely? What relationships leave you feeling depleted rather than energized? We can't choose happiness, but we can choose to take care of ourselves. We can choose to say no to those things that don't make us feel good. Just as we have the power to make healthy choices, we have the power to stop making unhealthy ones. If we want to find more happiness, that is.

It's not all rainbows and unicorns, however, even when we make positive choices. I did an hour of yoga every day that February, and I still felt moody and unhappy and anxious at different points throughout the month. That's life.

Most of us want to believe in cure-alls, but they don't exist.

I've spent much of my adult life searching for the one book, superfood, or habit to eradicate all my emotional or physical problems. If I just do yoga, I'll discover inner peace. If I drink more water, I'll be energetic all the time. If I sleep eight hours a night, I'll be less moody. Okay, that one works, but I'm still plenty moody. Healthy habits will always serve us, but they don't guarantee happiness, either.

Still, there's absolutely no downside to taking care of ourselves.

Along with choosing activities that stand to influence our happiness, we need to be more selective with our thoughts. Those, we can choose a lot of the time. Attitude matters in our experience of life, and a bad attitude never invites a good life. When I revert to viewing my reality with a negative slant, my reality turns darker. When I commit to staying open to the positive in any situation, my world glows brighter. I'm not suggesting that we pretend everything is rosy when we're stuck in a bush of thorns. But doesn't it serve us to give at least as much attention to the positives as we do to the negatives? When I make an effort to integrate positive thinking 50 percent of the time, the quality of my life goes up about 5,000 percent. That's a sensational return on investment.

Though the following has been stated four billion times, and we all know it in our hearts to be true, it's worth repeating: lasting or recurring happiness has nothing to do with the outside world. One of the great barriers to happiness lies in the stubbornness with which we seek it outside ourselves — in clothes and cars and husbands and girlfriends and TV and drugs and, and, and. Your happiness lives within you, not in

THE HAPPINESS CHALLENGE   133

the stitches of your brand-new jeans or the salary increase from your promotion at work. Have you ever felt miserable, even though things were going pretty well? Or content, even though you were out of work and late with the bills? I remember the day I got the offer for this book. I was sad that day, about the state of our world, and though I felt excited to get a book offer, my sadness stayed with me. Our outside circumstances affect how we feel, but they are not the makers or breakers of our happiness. That will always be an inside job. And happiness, like all the emotions, will always be fleeting, moving in and out of our lives. Staying for a while, then retreating, then returning again.

Life is about more than happiness, anyway. It's okay to feel all the things we feel. It's human. Consider everything we'd miss out on if we were happy all the time. My sadness has taught me empathy and compassion for others in pain, a gift I cherish as much as any other. My sadness also brings a depth to my joy that wouldn't exist without the contrast. When I really allow myself to be sad, I also open myself up to profound happiness. My anger has ignited in me many calls to action and has been the catalyst for countless moments of change. Even the threat of shame, which never leads to happiness, has inspired me at times to make different, more meaningful choices than I might otherwise have. All our emotions serve us. They all have wisdom to share, when we're willing to listen.

We all want to be happy, and we can use that desire in many ways to create a more fulfilling life. Though we can't choose happiness, we can choose habits and activities that make us feel good and relationships rooted in acceptance and respect that support the truest expression of who we are. We can choose to honor ourselves by taking care of our bodies and minds, and by being grateful for the innumerable gifts that brighten our lives. We can choose to be kinder, more compassionate, and more loving human beings, with strangers, friends, family, and ourselves.

We can make all those important choices, and we can remember that we are all connected — all brothers and sisters — and all worthy of love. If we do all that, we still won't be able to choose happiness, but there's a greater chance that happiness will start to choose us more often.

MIDDLE SEAT

boarded a flight from LA to New York and settled into my window seat in coach. The middle seat was empty when I arrived, so I closed my eyes and launched into prayer. *Please God, don't let anybody sit there. Please keep the middle seat free.* You know that prayer, right? I watched as passengers filed into their rows, my fingers crossed as the odds of an empty middle seat increased by the second. The aisle began to clear out. The flight attendants shut the last overheard bins. I swore I heard the boarding door close. *Thank you, Universe, for this generous gift.* I smiled and moved my computer bag from my feet to the empty space next door, then melted into the freedom of a neighborless flight.

"Looks like we got lucky," the guy in the aisle seat said to me. I thought I'd seen him praying, too.

"I know," I replied. "Empty middle seats are the best."

Turns out, we had celebrated too soon.

Kyle boarded late — really late. Over six feet tall and, I'm guessing, three hundred–plus pounds, he was exactly the last person I wanted to sit next to for five hours in already-cramped coach. If I had to have a middle-seat neighbor, I preferred a gaunt, four-foot-ten grandma whose size didn't in any way affect my comfort and who would likely have some hard candies to share. I watched Kyle make his way down the aisle, hoping he would find his seat before getting to our row near the back. *Come on, Universe, be good to me, baby.* No such luck. He stopped at our row and nodded apologetically at the empty seat. "That's me," he said.

This sucks, I thought. I didn't have to read the aisle-seat guy's mind to know he was thinking the same thing.

"Sorry about that," I said to Kyle, as I retrieved my bag from his floor space and brought my leg back into mine.

Kyle sat down, having to shove his body into the seat and shift from side to side to make his hips and butt fit into a space much too small for his body. I felt his effort but was still too self-involved to consider his pain. *No bathroom for me*, I thought, not wanting to ask him to force himself out of and back into his seat during the flight. *Now I have to be uncomfortable for hours*, I whined to myself, squeezing closer to the window and away from his belly, which had bulged onto the armrest.

Then my self-pity rumbled crueler judgments:

Gross.

How could he let himself get so big?

People that obese shouldn't be allowed onto planes.

I'm not proud of those reactionary thoughts, and they don't reflect how I feel. I didn't really see Kyle as gross and don't believe obese people shouldn't be allowed on planes.

That's ridiculous. We can't control everything we think, though, and I think mean, ugly, judgmental thoughts sometimes — more often than I'd like. Have you ever had a thought you didn't fully believe once you examined it further? Have you ever impulsively condemned a friend, family member, or stranger with a judgment wholly inconsistent with how you really felt? We are much more than our thoughts, thank goodness, or many of us would be downright hideous a lot of the time.

What matters most is how we choose to respond to our thoughts. Do we buy into our prejudices, or do we question and refute them? Do I simply allow myself to define another human being as *gross* because of his weight (or for any reason), or do I look at myself in that moment and consider why I would choose to make such a cruel judgment? My response to Kyle's weight had nothing to do with him. But what did it say about me? If we want to live in a world that better reflects kindness, compassion, and love, we have to question and refute our prejudices. Every single time they present themselves.

I'm not surprised by my ugly internal reaction, though. I know how nasty my mind can be, especially when it's inconvenienced in any way. A jackass prima donna. His Royal Asshole. I saw Kyle as a barrier between me and the possibility of comfort, so my mind went on the attack. I made him the enemy and his weight a weapon. So I sat there and grumbled for a couple of minutes in my head. To Kyle, however, I acted friendly and nonchalant. I'm much meaner inwardly than I ever am outwardly (my partner may dispute that, but he doesn't know what I'm really thinking when I'm mean to him).

Actions speak much more to one's character than undesirable, often involuntary thoughts. No matter what we're thinking, we can choose to be kind. Kyle already seemed nervous and uncomfortable, and I didn't want to exacerbate that. Surely he was having even less fun than I, smashed into his middle seat. According to every heavy person I know, flying is no party for fat people. How could it be? It sucks for those of us with average-size bodies.

Kyle and I chatted in spurts throughout the journey, about his hopes of becoming a chef someday; his desire to move out of the country within the next few years, to France, or maybe Italy; and his antagonistic relationship with his little brother, who was sitting five rows in front of us.

"He's such a pain in the ass sometimes," he said.

"All little brothers are," I responded, as a pain-in-the-ass little brother myself. "So are all big brothers, by the way."

I played the role of wise elder, and he acted the part of questioning junior. We enjoyed each other's company, I thought. I know I enjoyed his. As the plane began its descent, and I leaned my head into the window for a few minutes of sleep, Kyle turned to me and said, "I know nobody likes to sit next to fat people on airplanes, but I don't like being this fat, either. I'm not happy about my size."

My heart imploded.

I didn't know what to say. My wise elder wanted nothing to do with that comment; he grabbed a parachute and got the hell off that plane. I just nodded in response to Kyle, with my version of a compassionate smirk. I had no good words in that moment. We hadn't once discussed his weight or anything having to do with body size. His comment felt pointed, though — a clear acknowledgment of my discomfort with his body, I thought. Kyle could have been referring to the aisle-seat guy, but he was headphoned and asleep for most of the flight, so I doubted it. Had I done something during the trip to suggest my annoyance? Maybe a grimace when he first arrived, or a frustrated shift of my body to accommodate his? I wasn't sure. All I knew was that I, like many travelers, didn't want to sit next to someone like him. Someone fat. And he knew it.

I felt terrible.

I recognize the possibility that his comment reflected solely his own insecurities and shame around his weight and that I may have done nothing to provoke it. Still, I guessed that in some palpable way, my thoughts had taken over my actions, and I did something to disparage someone who already perceived himself as less than. That's on me. It's a lesson to be more conscious of my behavior. A reminder that energy so often speaks louder than words, and that both kindness and compassion require us to actively choose them. Though we can't own another person's response to our words or actions, I never wanted to add to his self-consciousness about his weight. I know the pain of judgment, and of shame. We all do. I spent years hiding underneath a baseball cap because of my prematurely bald head. I've refused to take my shirt off on countless beaches because of my hairy back and, when I have gone shirtless, have wilted under the stares of some who no doubt thought my body hair was gross. *People that hairy shouldn't be allowed on beaches.*

Much of my mirror time throughout my adult life has been spent criticizing my reflection. Most of us spend time attacking ourselves in the mirror. We're experts at it. No wonder we so readily attack each other the same way. I know, intellectually and in my heart, that I am beautiful as I am. You are too. Just as you are. That knowing, however, gets buried sometimes beneath a barrage of messages telling me otherwise. Billion-dollar industries thrive on us — especially women — feeling bad about how we look. They all say the same thing: if you're fat, you're an ugly failure. I can't imagine what it's like to be obese in the face of such ever-present judgment and abuse. In the face of constant shaming.

Though I hadn't intended it, I added to Kyle's shame. Amazingly, fat-shaming, so often these days, happens intentionally. Countless websites exist with the sole purpose of doing so. Entire blogs focus specifically on shaming fat people on airplanes. People like Kyle. It's become socially acceptable to disparage people because of their weight. On planes. Online. Everywhere.

At a dinner party I attended years ago, the conversation shifted to flying, specifically to uncomfortable flights. One friend mentioned sitting next to a guy so big he needed two extender belts in order to close his seat belt. Everyone's eyes widened in amazement, some in disgust. Another friend talked about being stuck in the middle seat between two obese people for a five-hour flight. We all grimaced, imagining how uncomfortable that must have been for my friend. We never spoke about how uncomfortable the flight must have been for the two heavy people crammed into their seats for five hours. It's as though we all felt they somehow deserved that fate for being fat, or at least didn't warrant sympathy. *If they just lost weight, they'd be more comfortable flying.*

Really?

Air travel in coach is not comfortable for anyone of adult size, and I don't think that's the fault of heavy people. I'm five foot ten and weigh 175 pounds, an average body, by most standards, and I felt cramped in my window seat well before Kyle arrived. Have you ever had an especially (or even remotely) comfortable flight in economy? If your answer is yes, I suspect you're the gaunt grandma I love sitting next to. *Don't forget the Werther's Originals!*

Yet there I was when Kyle arrived at our row, internally berating him for his size. He wasn't to blame for the airline's choice to sacrifice leg room and seat width in order to stuff more of us onto the plane. I'm fairly certain that if a group of obese people designed a plane's coach section, we'd all be a lot more comfortable flying. Kyle on an airplane was not the problem. My attitude toward Kyle on an airplane was.

When I consider my own prejudicial assumptions about heavy people, especially the unconscious thoughts that register before I have a chance to challenge them — that fat people have no self-control and are unhealthy, lazy, and self-loathing — I recognize that all these conditioned beliefs are predicated on the false notion that being fat is wrong. And that the only respectable option for a heavy person is to do whatever it takes to get thin. Cue the diet pill commercial.

Only, being fat isn't wrong. Shaming fat people is.

Not all heavy people are unhealthy, just as not all skinny people are healthy. Not all fat people are damaged or self-loathing or whatever other generalizations I've wanted to apply to them throughout my life. That's not the point, any-way. Regardless of the reason people are fat — overeating, hormones, thyroid, anxiety, body type, genetics, disability, or preference — it's none of my business. They deserve to be treated with kindness, and given the same respect and civility we should naturally be granting all people.

Consider your insecurities for a minute. (I know, fun!) Consider the shame you carry about some aspect of your ap-pearance. We carry this shame because we buy into some false notion of what it means to be beautiful, and because others buy into it, too. Others who may judge and insult us, adding to our shame.

Most heavy people already carry a tremendous amount of shame about their bodies. Actually, most everyone does. How many people do you know who just can't wait to ogle themselves naked in the mirror? Shaming each other further in no way serves any of us, emotionally or physically. We can't often prevent our prejudicial thoughts from arising, but we can certainly challenge them and stop ourselves from acting in accordance with them. We can acknowledge our own con-ditioned attitudes and commit ourselves to relating beyond them. Our world is not made beautiful when more of us are skinny or smooth or blond. It's made beautiful when more of us are happy, with less shame and more love for ourselves, and with deeper compassion and empathy for one another.

When I look in the mirror, I see a middle-aged hairy man with a bald head, a smallish belly, and a butt that's gotten a little flat. I see a forehead with wrinkles and laugh lines around my eyes. I see a large nose, an ever-graying beard, and deep-set eyes with whites that tint yellowish. I see a big smile with turned-in front teeth and a layer of crooked bottom teeth. I see skinny legs spotted with bald patches, and gray hair beginning to color a dark-brown hairy chest.

That's an objective view of my body. How I react to that view is another story. Do I see those traits as attractive, as ugly, or as something in between? And why do I allow how I see my physicality to play such a big role in how I feel about myself and the choices I make? I know that what matters most lives beneath the surface. Who I am has nothing to do with how I look. The same goes for each of us, and for Kyle.

That day on the plane, I met a kind, articulate, intelligent, sensitive young man with aspirations. None of that had anything to do with his weight.

WELL-TRAINED

During one of my apartment building's many air-conditioning *and* water outages my first year in hellishly humid, 10,000-degree Panama City, I escaped to the building's pool to keep from dissolving. That's when I first ran into Juan Carlos. He was at the pool bathrooms, where he sat on the toilet in the stall with the faulty lock. Thinking the stall was empty, I walked in. He panicked, and then I panicked, apologized, and ran out. I guarantee he never sat down in that stall again.

Later that day, I saw him in the gym, training one of my neighbors, a lovely Russian woman with a big, warm smile. They jumped, kicked, punched, and *burpeed* together, and even laughed some. I spoke to her after her workout to ask about Juan Carlos as a trainer. She raved and raved about him, then gave me his number. Juan Carlos and I met for a training session the next week. We've been working out together ever since. (Okay, that last line was a lie but it sounded so natural and romantic.) We actually don't work out together anymore, but only because I'd rather take naps than go to the gym.

At that point, however, I couldn't wait to start a regular workout routine. In Panama most of the bigger apartment buildings have gyms, so the personal trainers come to you. This convenience removes the obstacle of actually having to leave your building to get to a gym, which has often proven too big an obstacle for me. And each session was just $25, a quarter of the New York City price. This removed the obstacle of having to take out a second mortgage to afford a personal trainer. (Which would have been extra difficult because I didn't even have a first mortgage.)

Juan Carlos and I hit it off instantly. Like *hermanos* from another mother. He oozed enthusiasm and sincerity. You just wanted to squeeze him and tousle his hair, because he was that sweet and energetic. Like a puppy. A handsome, ripped, six-packed puppy. He took fitness seriously, and he believed that good health demanded a focus on body, mind, and spirit. A trinity of wellness, he called it. And though he was a certified ass-kicker in the gym, his training transcended big biceps and tight glutes. But you were likely to get those, too, if you did what he said.

We talked about everything during our workouts, from the mundane to the spiritual. He understood English better than he spoke it, and I spoke Spanish better than I understood it, but we managed. We got each other, and we laughed a lot.

Soon after we began training together, Juan Carlos started following my Facebook page and had come to view me as a wise *hombre*. He rarely arrived at one of our sessions without a question he'd been thinking about.

"Scott! Why there so much racist in *los Estados Unidos?*"

"Scott! You think possible for two people to be monogamy all relationship?"

"Scott! What you think is most important thing in life?"

"Scott! You been eat a lot of carbs lately, no?"

Yes.

I loved our conversations, and not just because I could
use them as distractions from my workout. I did that often,
though. It's really hard to do push-ups when you're recount-
ing the history of racism in the United States. One day Juan
Carlos arrived at the gym less bubbly than usual.

"What's wrong, JC?" I asked.

"I no understand people sometime," he replied. He then
told me about his lunch that day.

● ● ●

It was yet another horrifyingly hot and humid day in Panama,
when Juan Carlos, a sensitive and caring personal trainer,
walked into a McDonald's to have lunch. A strange restaurant
choice, to be sure, for a fitness nut to whom health was of
utmost importance. He wasn't there for the salad, either, and
kale had yet to be introduced into the Mickey D's menu. Not
that I'm judging. This fast-food lunch would prove to be about
much more than mysterious meat and indigestion, anyway.

Juan Carlos ordered a chicken sandwich, fries, and a soda
and sat down to eat in the crowded restaurant. While he was
enjoying his lunch, he watched as a young man, probably in
his early twenties, entered the restaurant. The man seemed
nervous. He wore tattered clothes and was clearly very poor

and most likely homeless. He shuffled from table to table, offering to shine people's shoes in exchange for some money.

The restaurant patrons sneered at the young man and shooed him away, as though he were a disobedient dog. Still, table to table he went, and rejection after rejection he faced. Some of the diners even yelled at him to leave. Juan Carlos grew angry at their reactions. His heart hurt for the man. He knew he needed to make a different choice.

When the young man walked up to his table, Juan Carlos invited him to sit down. "Are you hungry?" he asked.

"I haven't eaten in two days," the young man replied.

"I'll be right back," Juan Carlos said. He ordered a combo meal and returned with it to the table. "Please join me for lunch."

Several of the other patrons, still uncomfortable with the young man's presence, continued to sneer at him, and now at Juan Carlos, too. One of the customers complained to the manager, who walked up to the young man with contempt in his eyes.

"You need to leave," the manager said. "Right now."

"He's my guest," Juan Carlos told the manager. "I invited him to eat with me."

"If you want to eat with him, then you'll both have to leave," the manager replied. "He's not welcome here."

Juan Carlos stared at the manager in disbelief, and then looked around at the other diners, all of whom seemed to support the manager's decision. He understood this was not a battle he would win. He smiled at the young man. "No problem. Let's go." They grabbed their food, walked outside, and found a spot on the sidewalk where they could sit. There they shared a meal. Like friends. Like brothers.

● ● ●

When he finished his story, there wasn't a dry eye in the house, and by house, I mean my face. He shook his head and with a heavy heart said, "Look how cruel people is, Scott."

"It's true, way too often," I replied. "But look at how loving you are, JC. Look at the example you set. Look at the difference you made in that man's life."

"I just buy him lunch," he said.

"You gave him so much more than lunch, my friend. You gave him your kindness. He's carrying that around with him right now."

"Maybe," he said, thoughtfully. "Why you no doing your sit-ups?"

Damn.

I didn't know I could love Juan Carlos more than I already did, but that story added some juice to my affection for him. What a beautiful example of generosity, of kindness. His heart called him to act, and he acted. His heart called him to love, and he loved. I don't know how I would've responded had that been me. I'm confident I wouldn't have sneered, but I doubt I would have invited him to share a meal. I don't even know for sure if I would've given him any money for food. Sometimes I do, and sometimes I don't. More often, I don't. Too often, I pretend not to see the homeless person sitting there, asking for money, because I don't want to face the pain of his reality and the guilt and powerlessness I feel within it. Too often, I ignore the call to love our fellow brothers and sisters, even if it's just with a smile and an acknowledgment of their humanity. We don't have to give money to offer compassion.

In my workshops, I've asked people to consider a moment in their lives when they were touched by the kindness of another. I'll ask you to do the same right now. Think of a time when you've been moved by the kindness of another individual — a stranger, a friend, a family member, whomever. How did his or her kindness make you feel? How does it make you feel now, to think about the experience? Pretty good, right? When I ask the workshop attendees to share their moments of kindness, the examples typically range from the small gestures of a stranger to the overwhelming generosity of a loved one. From an unsolicited compliment to a donated organ. One woman mentioned riding the subway twenty years earlier and being unintentionally elbowed in the face by an oblivious man. Another man saw the incident and took the time to check on her and make sure she was okay. She still remembers that stranger's face and his genuine concern. This moment of kindness has stayed with her for twenty years. Thirty seconds of her life have warmed her heart for two decades.

That's how kindness rolls.

I received a message from a childhood friend a couple of years ago. In it she shared a story I didn't remember at all. She had transferred to my elementary school in fourth grade, and soon after her transfer, she was asked to read aloud in our class. As she read, she mispronounced the word *reservoir*, and another student laughed at her derisively. She felt embarrassed and ashamed. She told me I gave him a look like "oh come on, be nice," and then shot her an understanding smile. It helped her so much right then, to feel okay and to read on. That moment had stayed with her for thirty-five years. I had no idea. Just consider how many people you have touched   from elementary school friends to subway strangers — by your kindness. Imagine the many moments you've played a role in someone's happiness, simply by showing up with a loving heart. People are out there telling stories about what you've done for them. People you don't even know!

That's how kindness rolls.

When I consider the many mandates of love, kindness stands out as the easiest. We all know how to be kind, and we have all experienced the benefits of another person's kindness. We are given opportunities to exercise our kindness constantly. Through a smile, a greeting, a compliment. A phone call, encouragement, the benefit of the doubt. Every interaction with another person is an invitation to practice kindness. And every time we act with kindness, we serve everyone involved, including ourselves. Like everything else rooted in love, kindness feels as good to give as it does to receive. Maybe even better.

We know that our actions affect others, but we can't really know to what extent our kindness — or lack thereof — ultimately impacts someone's life. That's just one reason to make kindness our default.

When in doubt, be kind.

I woke up in a pissy mood recently, committed to gloom before I had even rolled out of bed. Still grumpy that afternoon, I went to the supermarket, only to be greeted by the sweetest checkout clerk *ever*. I couldn't resist her happy eyes and huge smile. We had a quick conversation in Spanish, much of which I didn't understand, and it didn't even matter. Her sweetness and enthusiasm completely shifted me out of my pissy mood. I carried her joy with me the rest of the day. Everyone I encountered later that day benefited from her kindness. I suspect the young man Juan Carlos shared a lunch with faces rejection and disdain daily. I have no doubt he carried Juan Carlos's kindness with him that day. Juan Carlos's generosity made a difference in his life, even if only for an afternoon. Perhaps, though, he'll be talking about Juan Carlos for years to come.

It's too easy to feel lost and powerless, like we can't make any real difference in this messed-up world. I've often become paralyzed by the amount of violence and oppression that exists worldwide, paralyzed by my seeming inability to do anything about it. But we are not powerless to effect positive change. Indeed, we are powerful beyond measure, each one of us, in our ability to treat each other with kindness. If you want to change lives, then be kind and patient with strangers, be open and generous with your friends and family, and talk to your neighbors — and listen to them, too. Don't underestimate the extraordinary effect you have every single time you show up to a situation with an open, loving heart. The checkout clerk shifted me out of my funk with her kindness. When my partner, G, got home that night, I greeted him with a smile instead of the scowl he might have gotten because of my foul mood. Our kindness transcends the moment of delivery. It affects more than we can ever know.

That's how kindness rolls.

Kindness acts as a magnet, by the way, for more of the same in return. When I walk out into the world with an open heart and a smile on my face, I invite smiles and warmth. That doesn't mean everyone showers me with their love, but more do than when I go out closed down and bitchy. If you don't believe in the law of attraction, start paying attention to your attitude and to what you attract in different moments. I find there's almost always a direct correlation. When I'm loving, I attract more love. That's a good reason to be loving.

Love doesn't just call on us to be kind in obvious situations, either. Sure, it's wonderful to hold open the door for a person carrying groceries, but can you open your heart to your partner when he's pissing you off? It takes no effort to share a loving comment when your friend posts a picture of her baby on Facebook, but can you resist attacking someone online who posts something you disagree with? Can you instead share your point of view without judgment and venom? I thought myself a kindness king until I had an issue with my cable service recently and had to talk to four different service reps to deal with it. I lost my shit on rep number 2, and things only went downhill from there. I became a self-righteous, angry, impatient asshole. One phone call sent me over the edge.

I want to become so rooted in my kindness that it's not dependent on the words or actions of others. No matter how they choose to be, I can choose to be kind. That's power. That's love. That's change making. I'm not there yet, but I'm working on it. Wanna join me?

Let's start with ourselves.

When we think of kindness, it's natural, and important, to consider how we can be kinder to others. But what about ourselves? Surely we're entitled to our own kindness. We benefit most from the love we have to share. With that in mind, how do you treat yourself? Do you offer yourself the same smile you would a loved one? Are you lifting yourself up or tearing yourself down? We have to look at how we talk to ourselves and focus on a kinder inner dialogue. We don't live in a world where everyone is sweet to one another. We're likely to face a good share of assholes out there. At the very least, let's not be assholes to ourselves.

Juan Carlos proved that it takes just one person within a room of many (or a world of many) to recognize when something is wrong and do whatever he or she can to make it right. His actions may not have inspired any of the other diners to act accordingly, but he certainly affected the young homeless man, who was the person most in need at the time. Though Juan Carlos left the restaurant feeling discouraged by the experience, the homeless man likely felt encouraged by Juan Carlos's decency and, perhaps for the first time in a while, actually respected.

One person acting from a place of kindness, generosity, and love can change everything. Juan Carlos was that one person. So am I. So are you. That's what's so powerful to consider: If one person has the potential to effect profound change, what can one family, one community, one nation of loving and compassionate souls create in a world that needs love and compassion more than anything else?

I don't know the answer, but I think we should do our best to find out. I think we should challenge ourselves, and each other, to show up in our lives with a kind heart. No matter what. Let's be the leaders of a love revolution, where deep connection is inevitable and ready kindness is the norm.

SNAPPED

One evening I sat on my balcony with a glass of white wine, watching the hot Panamanian sun set behind the swirling clouds I'd grown to love during the country's extended rainy season. For eight months of the year, Panama's moody sky delights in shifting cloud formations, as mild to violent rainstorms announce themselves at some point each day. Sometimes they last for a few minutes, often for several hours. I'd spent many afternoons mesmerized by storms coming to life above the distant mountains and then slowly, determinedly crawling over the city's skyline to let loose in torrents. Thunderstorms viewed from the fifty-first floor were a dark delight. Sunsets after such thunderstorms were positively heavenly.

As the sky shifted from rose pink to deep purple, my mind shifted with it, as daydreams sometimes do. For no clear reason at all, I began to imagine a large camouflage-clad man climbing over the balcony's ledge to try to kill me. I pictured him screaming at me, jumping on me, and punching me in the face, then pulling me out of my chair to throw me over the ledge. This scenario was not only violent and grim but also highly unlikely. I lived five hundred feet above the ground and didn't worry much about someone breaking in, especially by way of the balcony. But the unwelcome vision came, and I fancy myself creative, so I went with it.

"What would you do if a man jumped over the ledge and attacked you?" I asked myself. "How would you fight back?"

I'd never been in a fistfight in my life, except against my sister Kim. She used to beat me up when we were kids — a habit that ended when I was seven and kicked her twelve-year-old butt for the first and last time. Kim aside, combat had never been my go-to manner of communication.

I thought for a second and then answered myself.

"I would toss my wine in his face to disorient him and hit him on the head with my wineglass," I responded, happy with my instinctual reaction. "Then I would smash his head into the wall to knock him out, run inside and lock the sliding-glass door, call the police and attempt to explain to them — in what would surely be especially hysterical, second-grade-level Spanish — what had just happened." I wouldn't push the assailant over the ledge, I decided, because I wouldn't want to kill him. I'm a gentle soul, after all.

When I played out — step-by-step — this imaginary defense in my head, my mind sneered with disappointment. My ego told me I hadn't been tough enough and that I had looked too effeminate throughout the battle. Apparently, a man must never show his feminine side, even in pretend survival scenarios against imaginary attackers. So my mind insisted that

I replay the attack-defend scene differently and, like a good slave to my ego, I did. I sat before the setting sun, wineglass in hand, and pretended yet again that a large camouflage-clad man had climbed over our balcony to beat me and toss me to my death. Who says high-rise living isn't exciting?

The second time through, however, I sank into my most masculine self (which, arguably, might still not be very masculine). I didn't toss my wine in the man's face, like one would on *The Real Housewives of Beverly Hills*; I threw it with force, like one would on *The Real Housewives of New Jersey*. Then I beat him over the head with the glass, out-butching the less-than-manly knock on the side of the head I had utilized in my first attempt. When it came to ramming him headfirst into the wall, I went Incredible Hulk on his ass and, as though the planet's survival depended on it, crashed him over and over again into the wall until he lay limp at my feet. *Hulk smash!* I even entertained calling the police in calm, fluent, adult Spanish, but I just couldn't bring myself to imagine something so outrageous.

My ego felt satisfied with fight number two, at least enough to let me enjoy my last sip of sauvignon blanc and the final few minutes of the radiant sunset in peace. Like real men do.

Now, in actual life, I've got a bit of everything within me. Some masculine, some feminine, some whatever the hell feels right—inine. That's part of being human, of being free. We've all got it all going on inside — from Rocky to the Rockettes. We just tend to show the parts we don't feel the need to repress, the safe traits that keep our egos happy and society comfortable. Nothing to fear in the status quo. Accordingly, we hide the parts that make us feel embarrassed or insecure — even though they may be the truest longings of our hearts — the ones that don't conform to a lifetime of conditioning, the ones easier to criticize and condemn because they are too much this or too little that.

How often have you stopped yourself from saying or doing what you truly wanted to say or do because of the negative response you feared you'd receive? How often do we compromise our truth solely to keep others (and our own egos) feeling comfortable and secure? Allow me to answer that: probably daily, maybe hourly, definitely *way too often*.

We pay a price for silencing our truth. We compromise our health, our happiness, and our overall well-being — just to appear *normal*, as if there is such a thing. It's particularly difficult to find joy in a life lived in accordance with the limitations of our egos, when our souls so desperately want to be free. Our repression asserts itself as anger, resentment, judgment, and self-abuse. On a more global scale, through violence, oppression, and wars. Really bad stuff. Most repressed people, like pressure cookers, can only hold it together for so long before they explode in some way (at least I imagine, as far as pressure cookers are concerned, but I don't cook and can't swear to that). We hurt ourselves by hiding who we really are and how we really feel, and we do a massive disservice to the universal call for honesty and to love's mandate to be as authentic as possible.

Truth, though scary, knows how to heal.

Our world would be a more connected, much friendlier place if more of us felt free to be who we really were and encouraged others to live with that same sense of freedom. Imagine if we could become cheerleaders for each other's authenticity. Muses for one another's truth. In order to find the courage to be more authentic, we must first become aware of the ways in which our minds steer us away from truth and toward conformity. We are responsible if we buy into the conditioning, and the marketing, that demands we look and act like everyone else. We can choose to say no.

I succumbed to my ego's combat demands on the balcony and played into its ridiculous expectations of masculinity. Who's more macho than the Hulk? As that evening turned to night, however, my ego and I would have another confrontation ahead of us, and that battle would unfold quite differently.

Cue the bass drum, or the trombone, or the score from Jaws, *or whatever makes for a dramatic prelude to this next gripping scene.*

With the attacker down, the sun set, and the wine drunk, I sauntered inside and put on some music. As will happen, with or without wine, I started to dance around my apartment, shaking my booty to Michael Jackson's "Wanna Be Startin' Somethin.'" My ego, always wanting to be startin' somethin', joined the dance party and, like the scene on the balcony, wasn't at all happy with my moves.

"Stop snapping your fingers," it told me. "Snapping isn't cool. Snapping is something old people do — old people who don't know how to dance. Also, quit gyrating your hips like some deranged belly dancer. And what's with the raised arms waving back and forth? The roof's not on fire, homey; you can put your arms down. Don't even get me started on that shoulder shimmy. Really, a shoulder shimmy? You know you're a man, right?"

So I stopped snapping and gyrating and waving and shimmying, even though I liked doing all those things, and even though I was alone in my apartment, with absolutely no chance of anyone seeing me snap. Remember, my fictitious attacker was locked out, still unconscious on the balcony. He didn't know I was snapping; he didn't catch my shimmy. No one was around but me to judge my coolness. My ego still cared, though, wanting to stay in control at all costs.

I didn't just stop snapping and waving. I eventually stopped dancing, too, because now I was annoyed. "You're totally out of control," I said to my ego.

"And?" it replied. Irritating fucker.

"Well, stop it. I'm alone, I'm dancing, who cares if I'm snapping or tapping or twirling or moonwalking? Even if I weren't alone, who cares? I'm an adult. I'm creative. I'm free. I can dance however I want."

"No, you can't," it insisted, "unless you want to look like an asshole."

"That's a matter of opinion, not fact. Besides, you're the asshole," I said, rarely the one to take the higher ground against my ego.

"Maybe. But at least I don't dance like one," it replied.

My ego plays dirty.

But so do I.

"Okay," I said. "If that's how you want to play this." I turned the music up and completely let go. Snapping, twirling, gyrating, grinding, waving, shimmying. Cool, uncool, old-ish, youngish, girly, manly, I didn't care. I followed every im-pulse the music inspired. My ego didn't relent, not at first. It laughed at me, judged me, and called me names. It used my insecurities against me as it tried to make me feel stupid, ugly, and small.

"You're pathetic," it said. "You're a joke. You're way past your prime."

I just kept dancing.

"Really, Scott, you're making a fool of yourself," it taunted. "Nobody would find this attractive. You're better than this."

I danced harder, freer, more out of control.

"Enough! You're a serious fucking loser," it cursed.

"Maybe," I said, "but I don't care." I shimmied and snapped with abandon.

I let my ego have its say without having its way. I stopped paying attention to how it wanted me to dance, and as more time passed ("Wanna Be Startin' Somethin'" is a *looooong* song), my ego started to get bored with being ignored. And it quieted down, as it's apt to do when I get lost in the groove of my authenticity.

There's no home for an ego in freedom.

Just as there's no freedom in the house of the ego.

We constantly correct ourselves to fit some model of what we think is right or appropriate or cool or best, even when we're by ourselves, with no one around to judge us, with no reason in the world not to be 100 percent free. Even then, we repress our truth. Here's the thing: the rightest, coolest, and bestest we can be happens when we're being absolutely ourselves. Real, raw, authentic — however that looks and feels to each one of us. Even when it looks and feels freaky or stupid or strange by other people's standards. Real freedom — the kind that sings from your soul — rarely fits into other people's standards. And it never needs to.

Why would we continue to let other people decide what is or isn't true for us?

Why would we continue to allow our own minds — capable of wild intelligence and creativity — to prevent us from living our most authentic lives possible?

The answer, as always, is fear, and that's no longer a good enough answer, not when each and every one of us has the courage and resilience to make brave, true choices, despite our fears. Choosing truth is not a question of courage — which we are all born with — but of our willingness to be courageous.

Are you willing?

I am.

I'm not a fan of going to battle with any aspect of myself, especially my mind. We can't win internal wars, and we serve ourselves best by establishing peaceful connections with the fears and insecurities that populate our being. Sometimes, though, we need to put our ego in its place. We need to be clear in our commitment to truth and brave enough to act in accordance with our hearts' desires — even when our egos freak the fuck out. Alas, whenever we're living in accordance with our hearts' desires, our egos freak the fuck out. That's how it goes. Even then, we don't have to accommodate the ego's demands.

When the ego's working overtime to criticize us or push us to fit into some norm, we can choose to stop listening to it. Let its words become background music rather than a rally cry for action. Hear it without internalizing it. The ego will eventually get bored and take a break. Sure, it will return probably sooner rather than later to pester and annoy us, but when it's disregarded, it will rest for a bit. And there are few things in this world more beautiful than an ego at rest.

Authenticity is so much harder than it needs to be. It should be the easiest thing in the world to be ourselves and to love the truest expression of ourselves. But how can we truly love ourselves if we're not willing to *be* ourselves? Who is it we're trying to love, then? Some version of who we think we need to be, a portrait painted by the expectations of others? No wonder we struggle with self-love; we don't have the *self* part down. Maybe we'll have an easier time loving ourselves when we find the freedom to be ourselves, when we encourage our soul to sing its own melody, when we let our body flower as it's meant to, when we dance away from the mandates of our minds.

Sounds good, doesn't it? With intention and practice, it *is* possible. We can choose to un-become everything we've been told to be — or not to be — so that we can become everything we already are.

We can choose freedom.

After my ego had me Hulking out and resisting the snap, I snapped back into my authenticity. I checked in with my heart, the voice inside that assured me, no matter how I choose to defend myself against imaginary attackers or dance around my apartment, I am a fucking beauty, just as I am. You are, too, by the way. A fucking beauty, just as you are. No matter what your mind or anyone else tells you.

Perhaps it goes without saying, but I proceeded to shimmy and snap my way through the next several songs, dancing around my apartment like a wild, joyful, entirely free man.

JUST LOVE

A couple of years before this book rocketed to the top of the *New York Times* Best Seller list and I became a regular guest on the *Ellen* show (that's called "visioning," by the way), I self-published a much-less-talked-about coffee-table book called *Just Love*. Think memes, only fancy and in hard cover. Actually, I crowdfunded *Just Love*'s publication through Kickstarter — the most Brooklyn-esque of the many crowdfunding websites out there. I raised just over $20,000 in thirty days, which about covered the costs of designing and printing a thousand copies of *Just Love*, as well as packaging and shipping the nearly four hundred books I sent out to those who supported my campaign.

I thought the book turned out beautifully. So beautifully, in fact, I decided to throw myself a book tour. (Why wait for someone else to throw one for you?) I still had six hundred copies to move, after all, and an ever-growing eagerness to meet some of my Facebook community in real life. I organized readings at a dozen spirituality shops and bookstores from Detroit to DC and packed a rental SUV full of books. I announced the tour to my Facebook community — more than 200,000 strong by then — and hit the road, nervous and excited. I even ordered giant, customized *Just Love* car magnets that matched the orange book cover and only felt slightly silly driving around with them plastered to each side of the car.

Mostly, I felt like a badass on a book tour.

Then, more like an ass on a bad book tour.

Aside from a couple of packed events in my home state of Michigan, the tour didn't exactly draw out the crowds (euphemism alert). People may have been desperate for *more love* in their lives, but they definitely weren't clamoring for *Just Love*. I spent an evening at an Indianapolis New Age store chatting with the one woman who came out for the reading. She had driven nearly three hours to meet me (more time than I would drive to meet me) and was positively lovely; still, I couldn't help but feel disappointed that more people hadn't shown up. Was a crowd of two too much to ask for? A whopping five people came out for the Richmond event, at least, which is only true if you count the store owner and a woman who happened to be shopping for a birthday gift and decided to sit down for a minute. I chose to count them both in my final tallies.

After that Richmond event, one of my car magnets, apparently unable to handle the humiliation of another low turnout, dislodged itself from the passenger side door and flew to freedom somewhere along Highway 95. Who could blame it?

When the *Oogieloves* film bombed, I doubted my talent and felt like a failure, ultimately recognizing both of those uncomfortable realities as a natural part of the creative process. I have yet to meet an artist who doesn't feel like a talentless failure with unfortunate regularity. I learned that I didn't have to let those insecurities stop me from creating. I may not have been able to control how I felt throughout the writing process, but I did have a definite say in my actions. No matter what, I could choose to keep writing. That choice would always equal success.

The *Just Love* tour provoked me to consider some deeper questions: Was I really doing what I was meant to be doing in my life? If so, why couldn't I magnetize people to show up for it? I'd love to report that those questions rooted themselves solely in spiritual exploration, but they rested as much in ego and self-pity as anything else. My partner, G, was quick to remind me of the 200,000 Facebook followers who *had* shown up on my page, but perspective and gratitude never make the invite list of a reputable pity party, so I ignored him. All boasting aside, my pity parties rock.

The *Just a Handful of People Give a Shit about Me…* I mean…*Love* tour began and ended in Michigan, my home state, with Nicola's Books in Ann Arbor scheduled to be the second to last stop. I hadn't ever been to Nicola's and wanted to scope it out before the event, so G and I headed to Ann Arbor one night to do a little reconnaissance.

We drove to an uninspired strip mall on the outskirts of town and found Nicola's nestled between The Old Siam restaurant and Barry Bagels. Esteemed to be Ann Arbor's *premier independent bookstore* (according to their website), Nicola's lived up to their self-proclaimed hype. Much larger than

I'd expected and impeccably organized, it maintained the friendliness and charm of a smaller, more discombobulated indie bookstore. Established yet fresh. Iconic yet contemporary. I felt hugged by the place the moment we entered and could easily imagine losing many afternoons within its book-heavy walls.

We strolled along one side of the shop and chanced upon *Just Love*, beautifully merchandised on a table full of local Michigan authors and titles. I hadn't seen my book in a bookstore until that moment, and let's just say it looked damn good next to *Fish of Michigan: Field Guide*. After an extensive photo shoot of me next to the book, pointing at the book, hugging the book, fake-reading the book, and feigning surprise to see the book — like OMG, is that *my* book? — G and I sauntered to the back of the store, where a brick fireplace stood in the center of a cozy seating area with a sofa and some armchairs.

At this point I noticed the one other customer in the store — a man, around my age, dressed in khakis, a sweatshirt, and a windbreaker and wearing hiking boots. He looked like any number of grad students you'd find walking around Ann Arbor, which is home to my alma mater, the University of Michigan. (*Go Blue!*) The man sat on one end of the sofa, engrossed in a book. As I got closer, I spotted the orange cover and realized he wasn't reading any old book but was in fact reading…wait for it…*Just Love*! I elbowed G until he noticed the man, and we just stood there, excited and stunned. Of the thousands of books he could have chosen in that massive bookstore, including *Harry Potter* or *The Great Gatsby* or even

Fish of Michigan: Field Guide, he sat there flipping through *my book*. (Insert the theme music from *The Twilight Zone* here.)

I'm a nut for universal signs as it is, always looking for coded messages from the heavens to direct me to a more spiritually centered life. I once drank my own urine after meeting an octogenarian hippie on a beach in Kauai who credited his health to his daily pee consumption — he drank his first whiz each morning. Certain the Universe had planted that kind, odd man on the beach to introduce me to urine therapy (it's a thing, I promise; there are even books about it), I eventually built up the courage to drink mine. I don't recommend it. At all. Of the many awful alternative health practices I've tried (I'm talking to you, Master Cleanse), drinking a mug of my piss tops the list of poor decisions. Even oversteeped green tea tastes like honey by comparison. I gagged — and I do mean gagged — the whole thing down, though, stubborn in my desire for optimum health and mental clarity. Stubborn, but not brave (read: masochistic) enough to ever do it again.

In retrospect, I may have miscalculated the spiritual significance of my encounter with the piss-drinking hippie. That man in Nicola's, though — the only other customer in the store, with my book, at the same time I happened to be there? Come on, that was some serious universal magic. A sign, for sure. Of what, who knew?

"Go talk to him," G whispered, nudging me toward the man.

I knew I had to — the Universe wanted it — but I felt awkward. "What am I gonna say?" I asked.

"Tell him you're the author," G replied, matter-of-factly.

Incidentally, I don't think he was as interested in the magic of the moment as he was in me getting the guy to buy my book. G likes to pretend he's my manager every so often.

I walked over to the man and introduced myself. "Hi," I said, "I'm Scott Stabile. I wrote that book you're looking at."

"Really?" he replied.

"Yeah, I swear."

"That's cool," he said. "There's some good stuff in here."

"Thanks. What's your name?" I asked, as I reached out my hand.

"I'm Johnny." He locked his hand in mine. "You seem to know a lot of things. I've been having a really hard time lately."

Johnny and I talked for about twenty minutes. He told me he was homeless and had been living out of his car for the past two months. He'd been homeless for a short spell a few years before, too, but had managed to find work and get his life together. He lost that job, however, and had been out of work for nearly a year. In the past he'd been able to retreat to his mother's home, but she'd recently told him she wanted nothing more to do with him. If he knew why, he didn't say.

"I don't have anyone anymore," he told me. "I feel totally alone."

"I can imagine," I said. "That's really hard."

"I try to think positively, and I believe in the law of attraction, but everything's so tough right now, and I don't know what to do. Do you believe in the law of attraction?" he asked.

"In general, yes, I believe the energy we put out into the world is the energy we invite back into our lives. But it doesn't always work that way. Smiles occasionally get scowls in return."

I told him that sometimes life is really hard and unfair and that all the positive thinking in the world won't necessarily negate some of life's tougher blows. "I've gone through some really rough periods in my life," I said, "and one thing I've learned for sure is that nothing lasts forever." I reminded him that he'd been homeless in the past and had come through it, and there was no reason to believe he wouldn't do so again. I encouraged him to look into the many social services Ann Arbor had to offer, as there was likely a support system out there he may not have been aware of. "I know it feels like it, but you're not alone, Johnny. You're not alone."

I felt so much love for him, and I wanted to tell him, but I kept it to myself. After many attempts, I've found that "I love you" doesn't always go over well with strangers, as some people can't imagine being loved by someone they just met. I think we're always better off loving each other right away and then figuring out what we like about each other from there.

Our conversation eventually came to an end. He thanked me for talking, and I thanked him back. He congratulated me on my book, I wished him well, and we shook hands and parted ways. G, who had been browsing/eavesdropping nearby, slipped me a twenty dollar bill to give to Johnny. A thoughtful manager, that G.

I left the store feeling uneasy, like I had somehow failed Johnny. Life had put the two of us together for a reason. Had I blown it? He clearly needed support and love, and though I tried to give it, I walked away feeling like I hadn't really helped at all. My words seemed empty to me, almost desperate. That's often the case when we try so hard to say the right thing in a

circumstance where there is no right thing to say. Sometimes
all we can offer is a ready shoulder, a nonjudgmental ear, and
a wide-open heart. I hoped Johnny felt my love. If my words
hadn't helped, perhaps my energy had.

Then I thought of the unlikelihood of our meeting. For
that to have happened at all, some piece of the right thing
must have transpired between us. Life knew what it was doing.
Johnny and I had just shown up to support the plan.

Then it occurred to me I may have overlooked an important element of the connection entirely. I had been so focused
on what our interaction had to offer Johnny that I hadn't
stopped to consider what it had offered me — aside from his
openness and vulnerability, which were huge gifts. I'd spent
the previous few weeks touring through cities to minuscule
crowds, questioning my purpose. Something shifted the moment I saw Johnny on the sofa with my book. It felt as though
life wanted me to know I was exactly where I needed to be,
doing exactly what I needed to be doing. If I wanted confirmation, there it was, in that quaint bookstore, in the form of
a struggling homeless man who had been drawn, for whatever
reason, to *Just Love*. My heart, my love, my words were, in fact,
reaching people, in ways I'd never even know.

And what if they weren't?

What if my creativity and my words didn't touch anyone?
Did that really matter? How much of that responsibility could
I own? When I've felt my deepest call to create anything, I
haven't focused on the potential audience. I haven't dwelled on
the need to reach people or be talented and popular, or even
particularly clear. My deepest call to write, to create, to bring

something to life, has always come from what I sometimes call *source* — that peaceful place within that lives beyond the insecurities, expectations, and limitations of my mind. The source of my creativity, and of my love. Maybe it's not my job to focus on where my love and creativity land but on where they originate. To trust in *source* to guide my creation, and trust in life to do with it what it will. Even if that's not much.

I've thought about Johnny since that night in the bookstore. I've wondered if he's found a job and a home, or reconnected with his mom. I still see him dressed like a grad student, on that sofa with my book. I hope, more than anything, he feels less alone. The one thing that still sometimes nags at me about that night is the way we parted — with a friendly but formal handshake. I know why I didn't tell him I loved him, but I sure wish I would have stepped forward and hugged him. I think he would have been game for a hug. I know I would have.

CULT OF YES

I was in a cult for thirteen years. At least my partner, closest friends, and all lists of *cult warning signs* assure me that was the case. I still ask myself sometimes, "Was it really a cult? Could I, an intelligent, sensitive, and generally rational man, actually have fallen prey to the manipulation of a charming charlatan who deemed himself an enlightened master?" As it turns out — yes, and yes. It was definitely a cult. Which makes me a former cult member. As my one friend insists — and even suggested I include in my author bio — I am a cult survivor. Though true, in literal terms, it felt a bit much for the bio: *Scott Stabile is a writer and cult survivor from Lathrup Village, Michigan.* No. I let the cult define me enough when I was a member. I no longer need it to give me any definition.

My cult was not like the cults that make the news, the ones we are all trained to fear. No mass suicides, no killings, no gay conversion therapies. We lived in the Bay Area, not some remote region of the Southwest, off-grid from the rest of the world. The students lived "normal" lives, in our own homes, working whatever jobs we worked. We usually gathered several times a week, for casual get-togethers and *student meetings*, in which our guru (a.k.a. cult leader) sat at the head of the room, talked about enlightenment, answered our questions, and provoked our insecurities so that we could face them. Nothing insidious at all. On the contrary, our gatherings consisted mostly of black tea and organic snacks, world music, laughter, tears, and the courage to be ourselves with one another. I loved hanging out with those people. I felt at home; they were my family.

The focus of every gathering — and every day — landed on the guru, who set the tone and demanded our attention, whether or not he graced us with his presence. That's how I felt much of the time he was around — graced, blessed, lucky to be with him at all. As disciples to an enlightened guru, we had one priority, and that was to take the best possible care of our teacher — emotionally, physically, and financially. Everything else became secondary.

Though it's been seven years since I ended my relationship with the guru — and my entire spiritual community (a.k.a. cult) ended their relationship with me — I still can't totally wrap my mind around the experience. My heart, however, remains clear: walking away from the guru, and from the world he created to support himself, was one of the wisest and healthiest decisions of my life. One of the most difficult, too. How does anyone break ties with their family without suffering?

● ◉ ●

I said goodbye to the guru in an email with the subject line *A Hard and Loving Goodbye*. I ended the email with these words:

> These past thirteen years with you have been inde-scribable. Thank you can't begin to cover it. I feel sad about moving on, but I feel optimistic as well. Opti-mistic that I can move forward with all that you have taught me, optimistic that I can continue to become a more deeply loving individual, and optimistic that our connection will remain, albeit with a different look. I am optimistic, because love is my goal. And I will continue to pursue love. You have ignited and fueled a spark that I pray will never die.

I ended our teacher-student relationship in an email, be-cause I didn't trust myself enough to separate from him in person or over the phone. I didn't trust my strength or resolve. I knew he would convince me to stay. He could convince me to do most anything. He could talk me into believing things about myself I felt in my gut weren't true. I needed to leave, though. I needed out of the relationship we had built, one I no longer liked or trusted. I needed my freedom. What you can't see in those final words to the guru, along with the gratitude and optimism, is the overwhelming fear I felt when I wrote them, and all the uncertainty I invited the moment I sent the message. I knew I couldn't simply walk away, not without re-percussions.

I spent almost a year deciding whether or not to cut ties

with the guru. For nearly thirteen years, he'd been the truest father figure I'd ever had, loving me in a way I'd never felt loved by anyone. He played the role of best friend, therapist, and dad, and I'd become addicted to his love and attention — two things I longed for but rarely received from my own father. Along with still loving the guru and struggling to imagine my life without him, I feared leaving him because of two realities more than any other: that my closest community of friends, who were also his students, would abandon me for abandoning him, and that God would punish me for betraying an enlightened master (even though I sincerely doubted his enlightenment).

My first fear came true. After I said goodbye to the guru, he instructed all his students, many of whom were my closest friends, to delete me from their lives. All of them — more than twenty of my friends, my chosen family — did so overnight, without exception and without comment. No returned phone calls. No emails. No texts. Imagine being discarded by those you believed cared about you the most. I was crushed, destroyed. Only my college best friend of seventeen years — whom I'd introduced to the guru — took the time to send me a single text, which read, simply, "Nothing is okay. Please don't contact me ever again." That was seven years ago and the last time I've heard from her.

My second fear, that God would punish me for rejecting the guru — prompted by the guru's repeated insistence that those who left his life would feel the wrath of God against them — never came to fruition. At least as far as I can tell. If anything, I've felt more blessed than ever since walking away from his world.

Though I've missed him and the community that had become my family for so long, and though I still love them all, I've never — not once — regretted leaving. Few choices in my life have felt as clear.

I almost didn't include a chapter about the cult, not when I could easily write an entire book or two about those thirteen years. How could one chapter even begin to convey the breadth of that experience — all the love and manipulation and sorrow and fear? It can't. But the guru and many of his current disciples — my former friends — have impacted my life too profoundly to ignore here; for years, he and they were the main focus of my existence. *Who's going to drive the guru? Who's going to cook for him? Who's going to shop for him?* His comfort came first; his happiness mattered most. It would have felt disingenuous to leave out the cult. Like I was hiding something. Though the guru demanded utmost secrecy, I'm long over hiding myself.

● ● ●

The guru, who often described his path as *the path of yes*, scoffed at the suggestion we were a cult. "But if we were a cult," he said, "we would be a positive one. The cult of yes." As I saw it, we committed to saying yes to love, life, and ourselves, unconditionally. We shared everything with each other, and with the guru's guidance, worked through our judgments and pain. I felt proud to be a part of such a group, no matter the label.

If we were the cult of yes, then most of the yes-saying directed itself from the students to the guru. He asked me to move back to the Bay Area; I moved. He asked me to stop drinking alcohol; I stopped. He asked me to clean his house; I cleaned. Whatever he wanted, I did my best to accommodate. We all did. Because, as he assured us, all his requests were directives from God. He was just the messenger, the light that would guide us to freedom. I learned quickly that saying yes to the guru and yes to yourself weren't always the same thing. I trusted him, though, and I regularly ignored my instincts and desires in order to accommodate his requests. He asked, we delivered. The cult functioned, in part, with an enormous pressure to conform to the mandates of the guru. He made the rules, without compromise, and we followed them, without complaint. He had convinced me that when I said yes to him, I said yes to God's will for me. When I refused him, I delayed the possibility of my enlightenment. Still, I take responsibility for the choices I made, for all the times I said yes but felt no.

I realize how crazy all this sounds. How blind and irrational. If it seemed crazy in the moment, I didn't even care. The guru entranced me with his love, his wisdom, and his charm. He epitomized freedom in the way he spoke and acted — always himself, without apology. I felt alive, inspired, and so deeply loved in his presence. He was magic.

● ● ●

I met the guru for the first time when I was twenty-four years old. I worked with and had become close friends with several of his students, drawn to their passion for peace and love and the genuine kindness that emanated from each of them. They spoke of their teacher often, relating the countless ways in which he had changed their lives — all for the better. After listening to them praise him for half a year, I decided I was ready to meet him. I felt drawn to him the instant we hugged hello, and I spent many hours in his home that night, talking to him one-on-one. I understood I was in the presence of an unusually powerful individual, unlike anyone I had ever met. He oozed confidence and compassion. He wanted to know everything about me, and I felt compelled to share myself with him. I liked him, though his intensity scared me. His deep-brown eyes warmed yet unnerved me. When I left his home, I waited an entire year before I reached out to him again. I think I knew that I couldn't approach a relationship with him casually. A year after our first meeting, I wanted to take my spiritual growth more seriously, and I committed myself to being his student. I agreed to walk his path.

Though the guru despised religion, he pitched his path to enlightenment with an evangelist's fervor, establishing himself as its prophet. I fell in love with him quickly and couldn't get enough of the community that surrounded him. Everyone seemed so clear in their faith of who he was that I felt clear, too, and incredibly lucky. Like I had struck gold.

I worshipped him.

As with all religions, my cult rooted itself in faith. Faith that the guru was not only enlightened himself but also had the tools to prepare me for my own enlightenment, which was my greatest goal at the time. Faith that everything he told me or asked of me, no matter how difficult or provocative, was being delivered through him by God, specifically to make me more conscious and free. Faith that the guru acted without ego, with only my best interests in mind, even when his actions appeared to be self-serving or cruel. Faith that by serving him I always served myself — that even by folding his underwear, washing his dishes, and organizing his garage, I was learning how to be more precise and therefore more conscious and ready for enlightenment. Faith that by giving him money each month — frequently putting myself into debt in order to do so — I helped to create for him a more comfortable life from which he could reach even more spiritual seekers and offer more enlightenment to the world. Faith that his clarity, as he professed it to be, mirrored that of Jesus and Buddha and every other great teacher. Faith that I, and his other students, were impossibly fortunate to be disciples of one of the rarest kinds of human beings: a truly enlightened master.

For thirteen years I worked hard to have faith in the guru, regularly confronting and rejecting my judgments of him. He insisted he had transcended his ego, though his actions often suggested otherwise. When he cursed former students or raged with jealousy over an ex-girlfriend or refused to acknowledge any of his mistakes or droned on and on about his enlightenment — all signs, I thought, of ego-driven behavior — I battled away my criticisms. He didn't tolerate criticism of his actions, and I didn't dare bad-mouth him to other students, because they would have told him everything I said. We all told him everything we discussed, especially if it had anything to do with him. We kept no secrets from him. When

I brought up my issues about him to him, he talked me out of my judgments and loved me beyond the shame I inevitably felt for having them. When I judged him as unenlightened, I scolded myself. "I'm not enlightened," I told myself, "so how could I possibly know what enlightenment looks like?" Every time I fought my way back to trust.

His enlightenment remained paramount to my belief in him and his path. He sold himself on it, calling himself nothing more than a *puppet of God*. When he acted loving, wise, compassionate, and kind, I effusively bought into his transcendence. Even today, about 3 percent of my mind, still beholden to his brainwashing, thinks perhaps he really could be enlightened and that I've misjudged him horribly. Regardless, I'm still no fan of his path, enlightened or not. The other 97 percent views the guru as a fraud. A loving and wise yet manipulative and dishonest charlatan. A man much more concerned with his power and comfort than with the well-being of his devoted students.

He often asked, "What if I am a fraud? Would it make any difference to you?" For many years, it wouldn't have. He reflected compassion and love like I had never seen before. He pushed me to love unconditionally and to forgive without exception. Fraud or not, he encouraged me to own my power and inspired me to make love my priority. I will forever be grateful to him for those gifts. What I realized, though, is that it's possible to convey the message of unconditional love — and all that love invites — without also being dishonest and cruel, and without elevating yourself to a godlike status where you are never wrong. The guru had mastered taking credit for all things good without ever taking responsibility for any of the bad.

I spoke to the guru once, about a year after I sent my goodbye email. I wanted him to know that I forgave him for directing the community to excommunicate me but that I didn't see his actions as loving. He told me he had prayed to God for the biggest gift he could give me after I left his life, and God had instructed him to have my friends disown me. He never explained how that demand was actually a gift, and I don't know if he was lying or just delusional, but I didn't believe him either way. Second to losing my parents, losing my friends so suddenly and completely was the greatest pain I've endured. That level of cruelty has no place in any path of love I would ever choose to walk again. I do forgive him, though, and all of them. I will love them all forever, and I will always be grateful for the love they showed me. Like all of us, they are just searching for their truth in a hard and confusing world. I can't blame my former friends for putting themselves, and their teacher, before me.

● ● ●

The fact that you chose this book suggests you're searching for something more in your life. I'm a seeker, too. We seekers can't help but look for teachers to guide us along our paths and, ideally, make the journey easier than it might have been otherwise. Teachers play an important role in most of our lives. As kids, we don't get to choose them. Our schools assign them to us, and we're lucky when we get a few who leave a lasting impression. As adults, however, we decide whom we invite into our lives as teachers. We select the friends, artists, speakers, activists, mentors, and gurus we most connect with and feel will most enhance our lives. We owe it to ourselves to be as discerning as possible.

We choose our teachers, and we can un-choose them, too.

I chose the guru because I believed him to be the freest and most loving person I had ever met. I believed him to be enlightened and wanted him to show me the way to enlightenment. I loved him as a person, but I chose him as a teacher — for my healing and for my spiritual growth. In the end, I un-chose him for the same reasons.

It's easy to stick with teachers or relationships or tribes that no longer serve our well-being, that may even begin to cause more destruction than healing in our lives. We stay because we're afraid to leave the comfort of the known, even when the norm has become unbearable. We stay because we can't extract ourselves from the pressure to conform, even when our hearts cry out for freedom. We stay because we question our perceptions as false, even when our guts won't stop screaming the truth. We stay because we believe we have nowhere else to go, even when endless possibilities live within our choice to move on. We stay for so many fearful reasons; even so, it will always only take just one courageous decision to leave.

It's vital to remember that no teacher or tribe provides the ticket to anything; you are the only necessary ingredient in your growth. I am the only necessary component of mine. We get to choose the other players in our story. And, beautifully, we never stop growing, and our story never stops unfolding, no matter whom we invite to help us along the way. No matter whom we disinvite, too.

If you're not resonating with a person — or if she doesn't act in a way that aligns with what you know to be true and right in your gut — even if everyone else you know loves her, don't be afraid to walk away. Keep searching for a teacher that ignites something clear and powerful within you, that sparks a resounding yes. When we move on from the teachers that no longer serve us — for whatever reason — we create space for new teachers, new lessons, and new opportunities for growth.

I tried for years to make my relationship with the guru work, even when it had become clear that it wouldn't. It is possible, sometimes, to try too hard. And wise, sometimes, to walk away.

● ◍ ◉

When I left the cult, I also left behind the goal of becoming enlightened. Another wise and healthy choice. I cared so much about enlightenment for so many years and constantly judged myself as a deeply flawed person against the prospect of myself as an enlightened one, against the example of the guru. I spent years beating myself up for everything I wasn't.

I don't view enlightenment as a goal anymore, not when it feels so much like a stroke of luck. Like winning the spiritual lottery, and the simple act of being alive enters you into the drawing. I'd like to believe the more you work on your spiritual growth, and the more loving you become, the better your odds are of winning the lottery. I'm not so sure, though, and it doesn't matter to me anymore. When I chose enlightenment as my primary goal, I worked hard at being a kinder, more compassionate, more loving, and more forgiving human being, believing those actions to be the path to enlightenment. I'm still working hard on those things, not because I want to become enlightened but because I want to become a kinder, more compassionate, more loving, and more forgiving human being. They're worthy objectives on their own. With or without enlightenment as my goal, the journey remains the same.

Well, kind of.

I enjoy my life not chasing enlightenment much more than I did while chasing it. I'm more relaxed about my spiritual path and more at peace with wherever it ends up — wherever I end up. It's true I'm in my head a lot, struggle plenty, judge my process, and battle my ego much more than I'd like. As I see it, that's all part of being human. An unenlightened human. Pretty much every human.

I stopped chasing enlightenment when I finally understood that it was not within my power to realize it. Enlightenment is a gift, not an achievement. What is within my power is my kindness, my compassion, and my love. I work on those constantly, and they reward me every day. Their gifts are more than enough for me. If my fate is such that some divine force decides I'm to become enlightened, it won't be because I'm wiser and more peaceful than the rest of the world. I will have just been lucky enough to be born with the winning ticket.

UNCLE SCOTT

I closed the door behind me, tray in hand, and took in the small exam room. It felt like all the other exam rooms I've been in — florescent-white and unnervingly sterile, the aromatic scent of rubber gloves and laboratory-grade hand soap wafting around me. There was an exam table covered in that endless roll of tissue paper that sticks to your back and butt when you sweat, with stirrups attached to its sides, like alien arms, something I've only ever seen in movies — not too surprising, as most males make it through life without needing a pap smear. A desk chair sat beside the exam table, and a line of white cupboards and drawers surrounded a sink on one wall. On the counter sat a combination TV/DVD player, strikingly similar to one I had in the mid-90s, on which I watched endless episodes of *Seinfeld*, *Will & Grace*, and *ER*. I set my tray down next to the TV and stared at the little plastic cup and the lone wet wipe perched upon it.

The cup taunted me. *Are you ready?*

I picked it up, raised it to eye level, and nodded. *Let's do this.*

I looked around for some assistance but didn't see anything. *Seriously?* I started to sweat. The last thing I wanted to do was rely on my imagination, not with so much on the line, and Sam the Scientist (more on him later) waiting outside the door. Then I noticed a "magazines" label taped to one of the drawers. *Bingo.* I opened the drawer to a small stack of ragged *Playboy* and *Penthouse* magazines, likely as old as the TV player. I breathed away my germophobia and rifled through them in search of any male anatomy, but found only unusually contorted, hairless female bodies. These definitely wouldn't do the trick. Just as I was about to relent to my imagination, I spotted a lone DVD buried beneath the magazines: *Spunk Junkies.*

Thank God. Now, *that* I could work with.

I rolled the desk chair in front of the TV, loaded the DVD, and watched, with the volume muted (because, Kevin the Scientist), as a busty blonde woman hiked up the side of a hill, only to chance upon a shirtless cowboy repairing a fence. Here we go. I paused the movie, closed my eyes and, for the first time ever while watching porn, said a prayer that went something like this —

May I bring as much love and intention into this session as I can. May my sperm help my dear friends realize their dream of having a child. May it play a part in creating a new life. And may my sample fill at least three vials — the average — so that I don't feel like less of a man. Amen.

I unbuttoned my pants, smiled hopefully downward, then pressed play.

Let's make a baby.

* * *

The seed (so to speak) for that office visit had been planted several months earlier, with a text from my friend Gina.

> *Gina:* What would you think about donating sperm to Sarah?
> *Me:* Are you serious?
> *Gina:* You two should talk.

She didn't even bother to include any emojis, not even a little stork. A few days later, Sarah, a dear friend from college, sent me an email asking if I would consider being the sperm donor for her and her partner, Ryan, who was a transgender male and couldn't father children biologically. Sarah had failed six times to get pregnant with anonymous sperm and had never felt comfortable with the process. They wanted the sperm of someone they knew and trusted. Ideally, someone they loved. Though Sarah and I hadn't had much contact in the twenty years since college, we never stopped loving each other. So she asked me.

My ego loved Sarah's request. She and Ryan could have picked any one of their thousands (by my ego's calculations) of male friends as a sperm donor, and they chose me. *I'm a winner! I'm a stud! People want my babies!* Ego aside, I felt honored that they thought enough of me to want me as the biological father of their child. Humbled, too, that I could play a part in something so important. And once I gave it even more thought, I felt pretty freaked out (by pretty, I mean completely).

My gut response was "yes, of course." If I could help two friends realize one of their dreams, simply by masturbating into a cup, why wouldn't I do it? It was just sperm, after all. But it wasn't just sperm. It was sperm to be used in the creation of a child. Which would have made me some sort of father, even if just biologically.

There's the rub: I'm not into kids.

I don't want children. I never have, not really. Sure, my nieces and nephews delight me, and babies' smiles have melted me too many times to count. In those moments, I think "maybe." But those moments last for minutes at most, and my "hell no" quickly reinserts itself. I find little kids super cute and generally tedious. So boring! The stories that make no sense and go nowhere. The insipid questions. The repetition. Oh, the repetition. How do parents do it? I'm good for one round of patty-cake, that's it. And forget about peekaboo. Talk to me when you've learned *Uno*, at least. Better yet, talk to me when you're old enough to interact intelligently. I want to hang out with kids who can deconstruct *The Power of Now*, or at least offer some insights on *A Course in Miracles*. I'd settle for an impassioned discussion of *Game of Thrones*. That's probably not very kid friendly, though.

I can't begin to imagine what women who don't want children have to endure. I've felt like a monster because I've never wanted children, or worse, because I'm not even a fan of them. But I've never had my purpose for living questioned simply because I chose not to procreate. I've questioned myself, however. I've questioned the depth of my spiritual soul. How can a man so committed to love be so uninterested in the most lovable among us? Am I, in fact, an unfeeling robot? What does my kid apathy say about me? I think not much, other than I'm not crazy about kids. That's just how it is, who I am. We're not all put on earth to parent children. Indeed, we're not even all put on earth to enjoy them very much. There's no shame in either of those things.

But there I was, a self-proclaimed child unenthusiast, being asked to help create a child, one with whom I would certainly have contact. I talked it over with my partner, G, who told me he'd support whatever decision I made. He doesn't always tell me this, by the way, especially when I'm making restaurant or movie choices. "Not Thai again" and "No more superheroes" are his most common objections.

With sperm donation, however, he was on board. "But give it some serious thought," he advised. "I think you're taking it too casually. Once the baby is born, you might be more attached to it than you think."

I doubted it, but how do we ever know what we're going to feel about something until we actually feel it? Even *my* robot heart was likely to stir the first time I held a baby I'd played a part in creating.

My friend Kenny suggested I play out all the worst-case scenarios, and if I was okay with them all, then I should go for it. Good advice, I thought, until I considered all the things that could go wrong.

- What if the kid wants more from me than I feel comfortable giving?
- What if the kid hates and resents me?
- What if Sarah miscarries?
- What if Sarah miscarries due to my faulty sperm?
- What if the kid is born with severe birth defects or disabilities?
- What if those birth defects or disabilities are due to my faulty sperm?
- What if Sarah and Ryan break up and she wants me to become more involved in the kid's life?
- What if I want to be more involved in the kid's life, but Sarah and Ryan don't allow it?
- What if Sarah and Ryan die and none of their family or friends wants the kid?
- What if their rescue pit bull attacks the kid?
- What if the kids dies?
- Oh my God, what if the kid dies?!

That's a lot of worst-case scenarios, each one worthy of its own freak-out. I found myself spinning in a galaxy of *what-ifs*, a universe of fear. Isn't that usually the case with big decisions, no matter how exciting and potentially life changing they are? Our fear of the unknown lurks within all the bright possibilities, demanding more courage than we hoped we'd need. "How bad do you want this?" our fear taunts. "Enough to deal with all the disasters your decision will bring?"

The worst-case scenarios are rarely realized, and never all at once, but there's no convincing a paranoid mind that all won't implode. So I sat with my list. I considered each one of the possibilities seriously, and they all landed on the spectrum of uncomfortable to horrific. A lot of horrific, actually.

Then I thought of G, and the list of worst-case scenarios I considered as my fear tried to prevent me from falling in love with him. What if he loves me more than I love him? What if we don't agree on monogamy? What if he turns out to be a sociopath? (There was, and still is, absolutely no indication that he might be a sociopath.) What if he breaks my heart? What if I break his? What if he dies? Dear God, what if he dies?! Yet there we were, five years into a loving relationship, not without its struggles, and we had found happiness. The *what-ifs* haven't magically disappeared either, but their whispers continue to fade into the song of our relationship.

Sure, we can fend off the *what-ifs* by not taking any risks, but then we fend off any chance of magic, too. We also possibly invite the worst *what-if* of all: What if I reach the end of my life wishing I had been less fearful, had taken more chances, and had really lived?

I didn't know how I would respond if something terrible happened to a child born of my sperm. I knew it would hurt, probably worse than I could begin to imagine, and I suspected I would survive it. I had survived everything else up until that point, and there was no reason to believe I wouldn't continue surviving. I also recognized how unlikely it was that something tragic would happen to the kid. Pit bulls eating children wasn't an epidemic I was aware of. I lost my parents at fourteen, however, and my mind became buddies with irrational tragic thinking. If you're calling me before 8 AM or after 10 PM, someone has definitely died. If you call me more than once but don't leave a message, someone has cancer. If I don't get a text from G, a pilot, within an hour of his landing time, a part of my mind begins to contemplate life without him. He'd be relieved to know this is never a joyful process.

I listened to an interview with a man whose mother survived the Holocaust but lost most of her family in the concentration camps. He said it was perfectly natural for her to assume he had died if she didn't hear from him within an hour of when she expected to. Her mind had been rewired for tragedy. My parents left for work one morning, were shot to death, and never returned. This was not a hypothetical. My mind got rewired that day. I never even considered their deaths, and certainly not their murders, as a *what-if*.

But we move on from our most tragic life experiences, simply because life keeps moving on and we don't have a choice in the matter. The sun continues to rise, and we do our best to integrate our pain into each new day without it stopping us from truly living. My friend was mugged at gunpoint ten years ago, by two men with two guns (one of them a sawed-off shotgun), in the middle of the afternoon in Houston. She hasn't forgotten and likely won't forget the feeling of those guns pressed against her forehead, and the depth of fear she felt in that moment. Her brain got rewired, too. She's more alert now, more cautious when she walks down the street, no matter where she is. But she still walks down the street, and that's what matters. We keep living, despite the *what-ifs*.

Every important choice brings with it myriad *what-ifs* — a barrage of worst-case scenarios — some based on what we've already experienced and some based on nightmares we know exist but have been lucky enough to avoid. Will you let the *what-ifs* keep you from living, from taking chances? *What if* something truly extraordinary awaits you on the other side of those fears? That's always a good *what-if* to ask yourself, too.

This chapter opens with me about to masturbate into a cup, so it's pretty obvious what I decided to do. I heard my fear, but I kept coming back to one truth that mattered more than all the *what-ifs*: I had the opportunity to help two friends fulfill what was likely their biggest dream, and all I had to do was jack off into a cup. Whatever happened after that, I could handle. G could handle it, too, he assured me. Just no more Thai food, for God's sake.

● ● ●

G and I Skyped with Sarah and Ryan — they in NYC and we in LA — to talk through any questions we had. They made it clear they had no expectations of me beyond my sperm. (I'm certain I never imagined writing that sentence before this moment.) Ryan was to be the child's father, and I was to be Uncle Scott. They planned to explain the dynamic to the child at a young age, and they invited me to have as loving a connection with the kid as I wanted. They would be making all the decisions, however, which was perfect for me. I didn't unload my list of fears, because my fears had nothing to do with their choice to have a baby, but I did list my ailments.

Let's start with *hyperbilirubinemia*. It sounds horrifying but just means I have a high white blood cell count and turn a little yellowish when I'm sick or really tired. It's not the sexiest look, unless you're into jaundiced chic. Then there's my *Mediterranean anemia*, a.k.a. low iron, which my sister Rose says all us Stabiles have. When doctors do blood work and tell me my iron is low, I tell them I'm Mediterranean, and that seems to relax them. I spent three long years in my twenties with *cold-induced urticaria*, which is hives brought on by touching cold things. Strange, right? Iced drinks and cold bottles turned my hands into burning, itchy balloons. So I used napkins to hold cold things. Then, with the same suddenness of its arrival, the cold-induced urticaria disappeared. I've been napkin-free for years. I also told Sarah and Ryan that I went bald really young and was ape hairy. These weren't ailments per se, unless you dreamed of being a supermodel, but I wanted them to be prepared for a bald monkey child, in case they were set on a smooth Chris Hemsworth type.

Perhaps Sarah and Ryan thought I was just making up my genetic undesirables, who's to say, but they still wanted to move forward, despite the threat of a yellow kid who may or may not be able to play in the snow. G and I were a go too, despite the fear of faulty sperm and a pit bull mauling. Really, I had no doubt Sarah and Ryan would make wonderful, loving parents, or I wouldn't have said yes. I can think of a few friends to whom I would never donate sperm for fear of the parents they would be. Luckily, they live with that same fear and have no desire for children. Not everyone is cut out for parenting. Sarah and Ryan were.

By the end of our Skype call, the four of us agreed to try to create a baby together. Not long after, I found myself at the clinic, praying to *Spunk Junkies*.

When I made the appointment a couple weeks before my visit, the receptionist told me that Sam the Scientist (remember him?) would be there to greet me and process my sample. Sure enough, Sam the Scientist, a Korean man with a thick accent, had greeted me when I arrived. In fact, he sat about ten feet away from where I was taking care of business (wink, wink), at a desk on the other side of the closed door. I'm not sure how many times he's had to listen to *Spunk Junkies*, but I muted the sound, not for his benefit as much as mine. I felt enough pressure to perform without having to imagine Sam the Scientist listening to me in action. I already worried I might be taking too long and pictured him out there checking his watch, tapping his pen against a petri dish, and huffing in frustration.

Once I finished, sealed up the contents, and cleaned my hands with the wet wipe, as instructed, I handed the cup off to Sam the Scientist so that he could separate it into vials (using machines and technology, I'm assuming). Each vial, coupled with Sarah's egg, represented a chance at pregnancy. If the average sample fills three vials, that's three different chances. Obviously, the more vials the better. It had been nine days since my last, um, release (you're asked to go without for at least five days before donating, but I'm an overachiever). I predicted four vials, maybe five. It took Sam the Scientist a good half hour to do whatever it was he was doing in the back room (and I thought I took a long time), as I sat in the waiting area, my masculinity in the balance, praying for a minimum three-vial outcome.

Sam the Scientist reappeared and said simply, "Two vials."

Two vials? Oh, the inadequacy!

I stayed seated, stewing in embarrassment for myself, disappointment for Sarah and Ryan, and then anger at Sam the Scientist. *He doesn't know what he's doing*, I thought. *He just wants more money* — they charged $275 per donation, no matter how many vials come from it. *He's too conservative with his dispersion.*

I walked up to his desk. "There's no way to spread it out among three vials?" I asked.

He snickered. "Sample's not big enough. There won't be enough in each."

I slunk back to my seat, a defeated, low-sperm-count subman, and texted Sarah the news. She seemed genuinely excited, however, or at least used all those exclamation points in her text to hide her disappointment.

Sarah didn't ultimately get pregnant from those two vials, or from five more I donated. She and Ryan were obviously disappointed. Perhaps devastated would be more accurate, but that's their story to share.

I felt heartbroken for them, because I knew how much they wanted it to work. For myself, I felt that strange mix of disappointment and relief. I had begun to settle into the bright possibility of playing a role in creating a life, and in participating in a life I had helped to create. And yet I was now freed from the fear and anxiety of all those lingering *what-ifs*.

Mostly though, I loved my friends and wanted them to

have their dream come true. For those who want to have a child, there's no scarier *what-if* than "What if it never happens?"

Still, we survive, because we have to.

Every time we move forward in our lives and make brave choices, despite all the disastrous possible outcomes our fear will create, we signal a deep trust, a deep faith in ourselves to handle whatever comes our way. We are, each of us, forced to survive circumstances we would never have consciously chosen for ourselves. We're all dealing with the reality of some of our feared *what-ifs*. In those realities, however, lives our strength and resilience, our ability to handle the unpredictable and sometimes tragic aspects of life. When things don't go as we'd hoped, we're tasked to keep going, and to keep hoping.

We're challenged to consider, with each new courageous choice, all the beautiful *what-ifs* we may be inviting into our lives. So we just keep sending out invitations.

LIKE FREEDOM

At least once a year, I google "Amish schoolhouse shooting" and read about the Pennsylvania tragedy in 2006, when a man walked into an Amish school and shot ten girls between the ages of six and thirteen. He killed five of the girls and severely wounded the five others before killing himself. Though it might sound morbid to revisit such a horrific event with regularity, reading about the Amish community's response to the shooting always lifts me up and reconnects me to what I believe to be true — that nothing is unforgivable and that everyone is worthy of forgiveness.

Members of the Amish community didn't just forgive the man who shot their daughters; they visited with and comforted his wife and parents in the hours and days following the murders. Many members of the community attended the shooter's funeral, and they even set up a charitable fund to help support his family. The Amish didn't just believe in forgiveness; they practiced it. They lived it. They refuted the claims of an entire nation that deemed the crime unforgivable and showed the world what forgiveness looked like. I cry every time I read about their kindness in the face of such sorrow. I'm always overwhelmed by the breadth of their compassion, steadfast in my belief that human beings committed to love — without exception — can create the most profound miracles and effect the most necessary change.

We can love everyone and forgive everything, if we dedicate ourselves to that possibility. It's this dedication, above all, that stands to heal our world.

● ● ●

I have four distinct memories from my mom and dad's funeral when I was fourteen. I remember sitting at the funeral home, as hundreds of people paraded past my parents' closed coffins to pay their respects. The only face I recall is that of my classmate, Jodie Goldberg, whose eyes caught mine as she waited in line. She gave me a nervous, sympathetic wave. I stared for a second and then looked down at my lap. I also remember crying in a side room away from all the mourners, with two of my sisters standing nearby. I overhead one sister tell the other she didn't know how I — the baby of the family and devoted mama's boy — would be able to survive without our mom. I didn't know, either. How would I? How could I? The third thing I remember was the moment before my parents' caskets were going to be carried off. I leapt from my chair and threw myself against my mother's casket, screaming and crying so they wouldn't take her away. "Mom! No! Mom! No!" I remember shouting, over and over, not willing to say goodbye. One of my brothers, I'm not sure which one, pulled me off and led me out of the room.

Incredibly, I don't know if that last scene really happened, or if I saw it in a movie or read it somewhere and owned it for myself. I can see the moment in my mind and feel it in my bones, but there's a part of me that questions whether it actually took place. It feels much more dramatic than I knew myself to be. Of course, many things I thought I knew about myself changed when my parents died. I was one Scott the day before their death, and a different one the day after. An orphan can never be the same person he was with parents. The day of the funeral, and the weeks around it, are mostly lost to me. Still, I have that vision of myself, body pressed against her coffin, screaming, arms outstretched, holding on to a little more time with her. I've never asked my siblings if it happened, because I don't want to know if I made it up. I want my last memory with my mom to be real.

The last thing I remember that day was being in the funeral home parking lot with my three brothers. They were talking and smoking, as I sat on a ledge staring at the ground with one thought in mind: I will never forgive my father for my mother's death.

Luckily for me, I didn't end up keeping that promise.

● ● ●

The man who killed my parents was caught and sent to prison for life. He's still there. I have a vague memory of being at his sentencing with my siblings. I don't know *why* we were there, really. I'm not sure what difference it made to anyone. Maybe we wanted the judge to see our devastated family, so that he wouldn't be lenient in his sentencing. Or we wanted our parents' killer to see the faces of the seven orphans he'd created, so that he couldn't ignore the magnitude of his crime. Perhaps his sentencing promised the only closure my older siblings knew they would find within their grief; being present for his conviction provided a breath of relief within a universe of hopelessness. With mom and dad's killer off to prison, we could at least lock away that part of the horror.

Though that day remains a blur, my parents' murderer does not.

I remember his name, of course, and even his face, sometimes more clearly than I remember my parents' faces. Maybe because his actions, even more than my parents' up until that point, impacted most profoundly the person I would become. He had changed my life more than anyone. He had taught me the meaning of loss and introduced me to unimaginable grief.

He had turned me into an orphan overnight.

Even so, I forgive him.

I forgive the man who killed my parents completely and without reservation. I forgave him a long time ago, but not until years after he took their lives and uprooted mine. Not until I simmered in blame and rage and fantasized all the violent ways I would have loved to take revenge. Not before I quieted my fury by imagining his troubled life to that point and the saddened loved ones he would likely never see again. I forgave him many years ago, but not until I learned that forgiveness of others is the only choice that lives in love, and that love is the only choice I want to live by.

To love is to forgive. To forgive is to love. I don't see exceptions, not where my heart is concerned. I don't believe any of the justifications I produce for not forgiving. The only way something could be unforgivable is if I'm not loving enough to forgive it — if the darkness that lives within someone's actions proves greater than the light that lives within my heart. I'm not willing to accept that. I won't discount the strength of my love for anything, or anyone.

I used to think my parents' murder was unforgivable. For many years, I didn't even consider the possibility of forgiving their killer. It didn't register as an option, not when he'd done something so profoundly terrible. When I thought about him, which wasn't that often, I hated him, and I was fine with that. He deserved it, I thought. But it felt awful to rest in a state of hatred and rage. It hurt. I grew to understand that to feel more at peace with myself, I would need to find a greater sense of peace with him. Without knowing how I'd find my way there, I eventually considered the possibility of forgiveness. What did I have to lose?

● ◉ ●

"How do you forgive?"

People ask me that question a lot. Some have struggled to forgive ex-spouses who treated them horribly, while others refused to forgive friends who betrayed them. Abusive bosses, back-stabbing colleagues, selfish parents, thoughtless children,

corrupt politicians, greedy executives, bigoted neighbors —
all have provoked in us the need, and inability, to forgive. Is
there someone in your life right now you have yet to forgive?
Or someone from your past you refuse to forgive? Maybe you
don't think they deserve it. Maybe you want to forgive them
but don't know how. Maybe you've tried and failed.

I wish I had an answer that guaranteed success, but I'm
not sure a definitive path to forgiveness exists, beyond a clear
commitment to it. We have to want to give it in order to find
it. If we don't, we'll never really start searching. There are
loads of articles, books, and videos that promise to guide us
to forgiveness and that no doubt offer some valuable tools
to help us along the way. Still, all the best forgiveness recom-
mendations in the world won't make a bit of difference if we
stay committed to the belief that something is unforgivable.
We won't climb a mountain we have determined to be un-
climbable. Once we shift that belief, and truly want to forgive
someone for what he's done — even if that's solely for our
peace of mind — our desire alone will likely lead us there. My
desire has.

Forgiveness takes dedication and awareness, and it takes
work.

I know that when I haven't found forgiveness, I'm operating from my mind and not my heart, from fear and not love.
Which means I have more work to do, more truth to uncover. I
understand my inability to forgive means I'm lost in the hopelessness of the past rather than the possibility of the present,
a slave to blame rather than a master of acceptance. When we
continue to blame others for their past actions — no matter

how hurtful — and how those actions still affect us today, we hand over the power of responsibility for our lives. We give someone else control. When we root ourselves in the present moment, no longer victims to our painful past, we take ownership of our reality and eliminate the possibility of blame. There is no place for blame in forgiveness, and no path to forgiveness through blame. If blame were the path, I suspect we'd all be master forgivers.

More than anything else, I've found empathy and compassion to be the most direct paths to forgiveness. Can we put ourselves in the shoes of those who have hurt us? Can we try to connect to their struggles and pain and the degree to which that pain plays a part in the choices they make? I can't imagine actually killing another human being, but I know what it's like to feel such rage toward someone you wish they would die a painful death. I know what it's like to feel unworthy and unseen. I know what it's like to feel used and betrayed, lost and desperate. I may not understand what it takes to cross the line to violence, but I can certainly relate to all the emotions that bring people there. We all have everything inside us; we are all beautiful and vile, grounded and unstable, whole and broken. We are all human. When we understand that, and when we're willing to see ourselves in others, and others in ourselves — through the lens of love — we walk the paths of empathy and compassion, both of which lead to a greater possibility for forgiveness.

I worked hard to empathize with the man who killed my parents. No one who is operating from any place of self-love or self-respect could walk into a market, pull out a gun, and shoot innocent people. I tried to imagine the life he'd led up until he shot them. How much sadness and desperation must he have felt? How much confusion and rage? I connected to those hurt places inside me that I'm guessing aren't much different from the hurt places inside him, or inside anyone. I understood that, no matter how ugly and misguided his actions were, pain led him to do what he did. I settled into my compassion for him as a fellow human being struggling, like all of us, to find his way in this difficult world. Then, eventually, forgiveness found me. I began to notice I could think about him with love and compassion instead of blame and rage. Something inside me had shifted completely and resolutely. Love had worked its magic. So I forgave him — not just for myself, but for him. Surely he needed compassion as much as we all do, whether or not he asked for it. No matter what choices he'd made in his life, he was no less worthy of love than any one of us, nor could he ever be. That's one birthright we all share as human beings.

To forgive someone does not mean we accept, support, or in any way condone his actions. Forgiveness has nothing to do with another person and the hurtful or horrific things they've done. As with our kindness, compassion, and authenticity, our forgiveness can only be found within us and can never be dependent on others — whether or not they are remorseful for their actions, or have asked for our forgiveness, or are even aware that we've forgiven them. None of that matters, not according to love. Love compels us to forgive, no matter what. No conditions, no excuses, no exceptions. I don't know if the man who killed my parents feels remorse for what he did, or if he's asked for forgiveness. Those choices have everything to do with his own healing, his own heart, and nothing to do with mine. My heart tells me to love him, and to forgive him. So I do.

● ● ●

In one of my workshops, I met a woman who had suffered horrible abuse at the hands of her stepfather for many years when she was a child. Once the workshop had ended, she pulled me aside. "What if I don't want to forgive that monster?" she asked me, disgust and anger in her voice.

"You don't have to," I responded. "No one has to forgive anyone if they don't want to. That's up to you. But if you're still carrying around so much anger over the abuse all these years later, and if that anger is negatively affecting your day-to-day life, finding forgiveness may be the one path that lifts you beyond the rage. Forgiveness may be the one choice that finally sets you free. Maybe."

She didn't buy it. And that's okay. Forgiveness can't be forced, particularly when we see no reason to act on it. We can only forgive if, and when, we're ready to forgive, and only when we stop believing in the unforgivable. But deciding not to forgive someone doesn't make you a bad, incomplete, spiritually unevolved person. We do what we can do. I have a close friend who has no intention of forgiving her ex-boyfriend for all his lying and cheating while they were together. She sees his actions as unforgivable. But she's happily married now and has moved on with her life. She won't forgive her ex, but she doesn't think about him each day and simmer in rage over how he treated her. She doesn't give him that power anymore. The woman in the workshop, as far as I could tell, still allowed her stepfather to determine her happiness, even though she hadn't spoken to him in decades. His actions still held power over her. In my experience, the surest way to get beyond the pain of something we see as unforgivable is to find a way to forgive, if, for nothing else, our own mental health and well-being.

A willingness to forgive reflects a desire to take care of ourselves. We all know what it feels like to hold on to hatred and blame. It's the worst kind of poison; it clouds everything. The more we resist the possibility of forgiveness, the more we invite the probability of unhappiness. We allow for a toxic reality that only forgiveness can clear. By forgiving others, we lift the cloud. Though we may never understand why they did what they did, or in any way condone their actions, or want anything to do with them moving forward, our forgiveness untethers us from the negative bonds of others, and from the victimhood of the pain they caused us. Forgiveness opens the door to a different kind of freedom.

● ● ●

For many years after my parents' death, I couldn't forgive myself for not begging my mom harder to quit her job at the market where they were killed. I hated that she worked in a crime-ridden neighborhood, and I was often afraid for her safety. I believed I could have spared her that fate if only I had done more to convince her to quit. I still believe that possibility, but I don't at all blame myself for her death anymore. I've forgiven myself for not pushing her harder than I did. Only after years of condemning myself, first.

Self-forgiveness is tough, often more difficult than forgiving someone else. Self-everything is tough, isn't it? We can be brutal with ourselves. Self-forgiveness requires the same dedication, compassion, and love we show others when we forgive them. Can we be kind enough to view our own choices the way we would the choices of those we love the most? Can we really forgive ourselves for everything we believe we've done? Yes, we can, with willingness, commitment, and work.

We've all made terrible decisions that have created unnecessary struggle in our lives. We've all stayed silent when we should have spoken up, or raised our voices when the moment called for silence. We've all caused our loved ones pain, and sometimes even hurt them intentionally. We've all abused our minds and bodies, refusing to care for them in a healthy way. We've all thought hateful things about those we love and those we don't even know. We're human beings, which means we've made a banquet of bad choices and will likely make plenty more in the future. All fodder for self-forgiveness.

If you have forgiven yourself for anything, then it's in you to forgive yourself for everything. The compassion you've shown others, you must show yourself. If you believe in God, then you are a child of God, and as such, you are as worthy of love and forgiveness as anyone who has ever lived. If you don't believe in God, then you are a child of Nature, and as such, you are as worthy of love and forgiveness as anyone who has ever lived.

Nothing you have done, in your entire life, lives outside the bounds of forgiveness. Nothing. If you haven't already, it's time to forgive yourself. For everything.

● ● ●

Imagine carrying such a depth of love and compassion for humanity that no matter what someone did to you or anyone else — no matter how horrible or hurtful — you could look him or her in the eyes and with sincerity declare: "I love you, and I forgive you. I feel your pain as I feel mine, and I recognize your need to heal as much as I recognize my own." I believe that potential lives within each of us, and within that potential miracles blossom, and humanity changes.

Their daughters' murders forced the Pennsylvania Amish community to face the conviction of their beliefs, and they chose to forgive. My parents' murder forced me to face a circumstance that most, including myself, had deemed unforgivable, and yet, with a deep commitment to love, I found my way to forgiveness. What a gift it was to know I could make that choice and that I can continue to choose forgiveness moving forward.

Forgiveness is one of the greatest gifts we can give ourselves and each other. It is one of the mandates of love, and one of the cornerstones of freedom. Mine and yours.

● ● ●

I forgave my father, for insisting that my mother work in such a dangerous environment, the same way I forgave their killer — by doing my best to put myself in my father's shoes and connect with him, not as my dad, but as another human being doing what he could to make a living and to make sense of our crazy world. He made so many awful choices as a father and a husband, but I know he never wanted harm to come to any of us, most certainly not my mom. Though I couldn't connect to many of his decisions, I could connect to his humanity, and with compassion, I forgave him.

Hundreds of cars lined up at my parents' funeral. The procession stretched for blocks. My mom and dad touched many people, from all walks of life. I don't think I fully understood their impact until I saw the number of family and friends who showed up to mourn them. I didn't know just how generous they had been with their support and their love. I wouldn't realize, for many years, that perhaps the greatest lesson they taught me — by example — was to accept and respect whomever crossed your path and to be a compassionate friend to those in need.

That lesson, like my parents, will live on in me forever.

ACKNOWLEDGMENTS

Thank you, Goran, for loving me so much and for letting me love you back. And for letting me write whatever I wanted about you. You make everything sweeter; you have since day one. I adore you and *ja te volim mucho*.

Thank you, family — Russell, Jimmy, Jamie, Todd, Fred, Rhiannon, Rose, Joe, Joey, Jen, Avery, Elle, Reid, Stacey, Paul, Nick, Kim, Phil, Camerin, Alex, Maria, Matthew — for being the most loving and accepting tribe I can imagine. I am so lucky to have you all in my life. (Don't worry, you won't have to wrap and pack any of these books.)

Thank you, friends, for being who you are, in my life and in our world. You are too many to name (and I would hate to forget anyone), so if you think I may be referring to you, I most certainly am.

Thank you, Stephen D. and Jason C., for always keeping it real and for being as thrilled as I've been about this ride.

Thank you, Abby, for your unconditional everything, and for your *buberlicious* giggle.

Thank you, Vando, Snjezana, and Igor, for the laughter, the love, and for making me one of your own.

Thank you, Susan, for your enthusiasm, insight, and dedication. You helped make this book so much better.

Thank you, Jason G., for your excitement, your instincts, your belief in my work, and for your easy way of doing things. I'm certain you've spoiled me.

Thank you, New World Library, for inviting me into your lovely world, one I've long respected and admired.

Thank you, Glennon, for setting one of the bravest examples of love I've ever seen and for sticking to it.

Thank you, Facebook community, for being there every single day, and for making this whole dream possible.

ABOUT THE AUTHOR

Scott Stabile has amassed a sizable Facebook following with his inspirational and provocative quotes, essays, and live videos. His previous works include *Just Love*, *Iris*, and the *Li'l Pet Hospital* series. Scott also wrote a feature film entitled *The Oogieloves in the Big Balloon Adventure*. A regular contributor to the *Huffington Post*, Scott runs daylong empowerment workshops nationally and internationally. He lives in his home state of Michigan with his partner. Learn more about how Scott spreads BIG LOVE at www.scottstabile.com or fb.com/scottfrankstabile.